HE SAT DOWN

TODD SMITH

ISBN: 978-1-59684-940-2

Printed by Derek Press, Cleveland Tennessee

DEDICATION

I devote this work to my wife Karen, who relentlessly follows Jesus and His ways.

You are unique and definitely one of a kind. Your insatiable hunger to know His Word is stunning and unparalleled. Your commitment to teach the Word correctly is refreshing. You aim to know the truth regardless of how long it takes you to discover it - you dig for the nuggets! Because of your relentless pursuit you have lead thousands into greater understanding of Jesus and His Word. You have left a mark on those you have taught. Thank you for not being average or settling for mediocrity. I have never seen anyone more zealous and committed to the cause of Christ as you. You are ever mindful of His heartbeat. Your spirit is contagious!

This book is you. Ever since you decided to follow Him your body is His body. You have been standing faithfully.

I thank you, our boys thank you and our Church thanks you!

Honey, you are covered with the Rabbi's dust.

ACKNOWLEDGMENTS

My two boys, Ty and Ethan, for the joy they have brought to my life. They are the greatest of young men who make me proud to be their Dad.

My Mom, I have watched you live with courage, fire and charm since the love of your life, my Dad, passed. He is proud of how you have lived without him. He watches all of us and is cheering us to finish strong.

My Church, Christ Fellowship Church, my family loves our tribe. Words cannot describe the blessing you have been. It is such an honor to do life with you.

My Staff and Elders, the Lord has blessed us with some of the greatest friends in our staff and elders. Life is sweeter because of our friendship. Thank you for allowing me to pursue God's calling on my life.

Sherrie Potts, Dana Fowler and Janet Ericsson thank you for your loving editorial work on this book.

Marty Darracott for his encouragement, friendship, and creativity in designing the book cover.

Table of Contents

1.

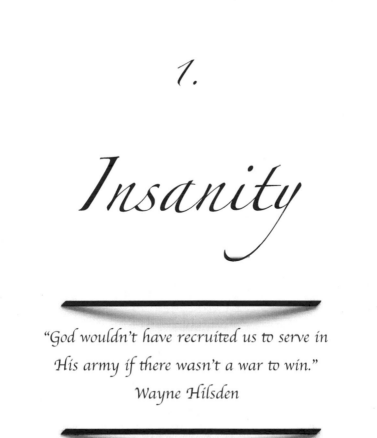

Insanity

"God wouldn't have recruited us to serve in
His army if there wasn't a war to win."
Wayne Hilsden

Have you ever walked away from someone you just met and thought to yourself "that person is a little crazy?" You know, the guy people describe as, not the sharpest knife in the drawer, three french fries short of a happy meal, or his antenna doesn't pick up all the channels.

Honestly, I am a little concerned you may feel that way about me after reading the next few statements. But, by the end of the chapter I hope you change your mind and realize that my elevator does go all the way to the top and there is no reason to ship me off to the ministerial funny farm.

I want to introduce you to an epic universal struggle that most Christians have difficulty understanding. It's a problematic dichotomy to say the least. Here it is. On the one hand, we are completely dependent and rely on God for our very existence, life, sustenance, our EVERYTHING. Consequently, what makes this so interesting and compelling is that God, by His choice, has chosen to be DEPENDENT upon man. Yep, you read that right! God is reliant and dependent upon man—you and me.

Honestly, in all my years of living on the earth not once have I heard a preacher say from the pulpit that "God needs man." I completely understand this belief is more than a little controversial; some would even say it is borderline blasphemous. But, the concept that "God needs man," as difficult as it is to embrace, is scripturally sound.

Now, for you to completely understand the idea that God "NEEDS" you, I feel it is necessary for me to start with a healthy biblical perspective of the splendor and greatness of God.

HERE IT GOES...

Our Bible teaches us that God is the absolute embodiment of perfection and beauty. Our great King is omnipotent, omniscient, and omnipresent. He is in the past, present and future, simultaneously. Amazingly, God transcends all time and space, and He is now present at all points because everything has its existence in Him (Colossians 1:17).

God is completely self-existent. He had no creator; He has always existed. He is entirely self-sufficient. Furthermore, He can do whatever He wants, whenever He wants to do it. He has no constraints. NO force on or below the earth can match Him, stop Him or control Him. No one can duplicate His strength, and His fierce power no mere mortal can contain.

Let me continue. God has no equal, not even close. The forces of nature obey His every order. Every creature fears Him. The demons of hell shutter at the mere whisper of His name. The mountains melt like wax in His presence. The earth shakes as He approaches. Angels bow before Him. Sickness leaves at His word. Death retreats at His rebuke. Waters divide at His command.

There is more. The Elders referenced in the book of Revelation worship Him. Twenty-four hours a day one hundred million angels make up the heavenly choir that continuously sing His praises.

Nothing can match the beauty and majesty of God. He sits on a throne in a realm beyond all earthly thrones, in a Kingdom with no boundaries. If His throne is beyond imagining, His glory is even more so. With unparalleled wisdom, He is faultless in mercy, limitless in love. His compassion has no end.

His holiness is not just an attribute. Holiness is who He is.

Our finite language and words are inadequate to describe and define Him. He has zero flaws. His holiness is not just an attribute. Holiness is who He is. He has no contemporary. He is in a league by Himself. He is entirely superior to all. This is God. This is our God!

Now to the puzzling part and the statements that could cause you to call me flaky and give you a reason to think I am insane.

Our God, Jehovah, the King of Kings, the Creator, All Sufficient One, with all strength and might at His disposal *needs us*. Whoa!

I know what you are thinking, "How can you make such a proclamation? God doesn't need anyone. The detailed description above proves He is all powerful and all sufficient."

Here is the sobering answer and the fabric of this book: History reveals and the Bible supports, from Genesis to Revelation to even now, God has *chosen* to place Himself in a position to *partner* with humans for His redemptive purposes. Therefore, He needs us.

LET ME EXPLAIN

The Scriptures reveal that God decided to *authorize and commission* us, even as fallen humanity, with the task of sharing His soul-saving message with every person in the world (Matthew 18:19, 20).

God has given us, the New Testament Church, the responsibility of carrying out His work on the earth, all of it. Every detail of it. In short, He is *dependent* on us.

Not convinced? Check this verse out.

1 Thessalonians 2:4
*"But as we have been approved by God to be **entrusted with the gospel**, even so we speak, not as pleasing men,*
but God who tests our hearts."
(emphasis added)

Read the verse again. Take a long look at it. Say it. Don't leave it until you grasp its implications.

It says, Paul and his fellow believers were **"entrusted with the gospel."**

Entrusted with the Gospel.

What exactly does it mean to be entrusted with something? This is how the Merriam-Webster dictionary defines *entrust:*

> *to give someone the **responsibility** of doing something or of **caring** for someone or **something**.*

In the original language the word used for entrust is *pisteuo*; this is the same word used for faith. In this text it is translated, "to commit to one's trust."[1] God is saying, "I have faith in you, therefore, I am committing and entrusting the gospel into your care. Share it with the world."

God PUT the Gospel in Paul's care...and said, "Share it with the world."

Like many parents, our two boys are our world. It is amazing how much you can love your children. A few years ago Karen and I celebrated an anniversary by taking a lengthy trip overseas. Before we committed to going, we had two main issues to settle. One, can we bear to be away from our children for that many days and, second, who could we trust to take care of them? As many of you

---

[1] Blue Letter Bible. "Strong's G4100 - *pisteuo*." https://www.blueletterbible.org/lang/Lexicon/Lexicon.cfm?strongs=G4100&t=KJV.

know, raising your own boys is no easy task, much less someone else's. We knew whoever we chose would have their hands full, so we chose carefully.

Before we left for the airport, we literally placed our most precious possessions in the hands of our friends. We "entrusted" our boys to them and "trusted" them to care for, feed, and protect them until we returned.

God did the exact same thing with the message of the gospel. He delegated to Paul the responsibility of "caring for" and "doing something" with the story of Jesus. In other words, God PUT the gospel in Paul's care. Whatever you do, don't miss the significance of this transfer of duty and authority. He placed the precious message of the entire gospel narrative in the hands of Paul and said, "Share it with the world."

Mind you, this is the same omnipotent God we described above. The God who needs no one reached down to man and partnered with him. In doing so God, in a sense, limited what His role would be in spreading the gospel. Thus, the impact of the gospel on the world would be directly linked to man's obedience in sharing the "good news."

> ...the impact the gospel on the world would be directly linked to man's obedience in sharing the "good news."

When one takes a closer look, the Bible is clear in that God exclusively gave man the assignment of communicating His love and salvation plan to men.

> *He put that message and the well-being of the gospel into the hands of clay-humans, mere mortals, us.*

Read on.

Paul left no room for misunderstanding when he emphasized again in 2 Corinthians 5:18-19, the strategic partnership God would have with man in sharing His good news.

*"Now all things are of God, who has reconciled us to Himself through Jesus Christ, and has **GIVEN** us the **ministry of reconciliation"***
(emphasis added).

Paul adds in the very next verse 19:

*"that is, that God was in Christ reconciling the world to Himself, not imputing their trespasses to them, and has **COMMITTED** to us the word of reconciliation."*
(emphasis added)

God has **"GIVEN"** and **"COMMITTED"** to us the ministry of leading unsaved men to Him. This means God has set the gospel message and the spreading of such message into our care.

Amazingly, the gospel is *NOW* exclusively in our custody! The beautiful gospel story has been delicately deposited into our hands.

The depth of this transferral of responsibility is extraordinary.

Think about what God did with the most important series of events to ever take place in the history of the world - the birth, life of, death and resurrection of Jesus - He put that message, the gospel, and the well-being of the gospel into hands of clay-humans, mere mortals, us. To me, this is a brain twister. Honestly, beyond reason. It seems like a risky move and a big gamble on God's part.

If you want to know the truth, in my opinion, it makes as much sense as a CEO of a Fortune 500 Company leaving the future of that company in the hands of a bunch of whinny, immature twelve-year-olds. No one in their right mind would ever think about doing such a thing, would they? It would be insane. Incredible. Crazy. Irresponsible. Unbelievable. Well, Jesus tried to warn us in Matthew 25:14f that that was exactly what He was going to do. He was leaving "the Company," His Church, its advancement, and ultimately its success to us, His children.

Frankly, I don't completely understand why He did this. He knows us, humanity. It's not like He doesn't have access to our resume'.

OUR TRACK RECORD

He knew man's history. We were and are ordinary, not-too-dependable, run-of-the-mill people, up one minute down the next. One week on fire for God, the next lukewarm. We are average folk who have time-and-time again proven we are not that reliable. Honestly, as humans, all of us are wobbly. Need proof?

For starters let us not forget our not-so-great beginning where we totally blew it. You know the forbidden fruit scene.

Our tremendous start didn't stay tremendous for long. Literally, the world was ours. God left us in charge. He wanted us to manage it all and have dominion over everything (Genesis 1:26-28). Paradise and perfection were ours to enjoy. Well, one bite of a forbidden
14

piece of fruit ruined it for all of us. Our first opportunity to demonstrate our superiority, greatness and dependability didn't end well.

How about the flight-out-of-Egypt episode? All we had to do was march straight for three to four weeks, keep our mouths shut and we would have made it into the Promised Land, the land flowing with milk and honey, paradise. But no, we couldn't hold it together. We grumbled about the food. We whined about the sleeping conditions; we griped about the humidity, we complained about who was in charge, and deplored the hot summer days. We even dreamt of the good ole' days of slavery where we made bricks with straw and mud. And to top it off, in the desert on our way to "paradise" we built a golden calf to worship. That was a big no-no.

We lost our focus. And boy it cost us dearly: circling the wilderness for 40 long years. And as an added footnote, everyone died on the way except for a few faith-filled people. Yep, not good.

For hundreds of years the soap opera was predictable: brief periods of obedience followed by complaining, rebellion, fear, remorse, then obedience followed by … well, you know.

Need further confirmation that humankind is temperamental and unpredictable? How about Judas' betrayal? How about when Jesus is dying, just one disciple, one follower, one friend is there-John.

Does Peter whacking a dude's ear off in the Garden, denying Christ around the campfire, then returning to his fishing career ring a bell? And of course, there is Thomas the doubter who wouldn't believe unless he touched Jesus' nail-pierced hands.

These are our people. We are these people and their story is our story. Sadly, this has been our modus operandi since the beginning.

Yes, from time to time moments of promise and flashes of faithfulness can be seen. For example, Abraham was willing to sacrifice his beloved son Isaac. David slew the giant. Joshua and Caleb believed they could conquer all. Esther boldly approached the King on behalf of her people. Noah built the ark. Peter walked on the water. John went all the way to the cross with Jesus.

It is true we have had times of being nearly flawless, impeccable and brilliant. However, in my opinion, to give us carte-blanche responsibility of the well-being of the Gospel may be a bit much. If I were God, and having a clear understanding of man's reputation, I wouldn't have done it. No way! But, He chose to. This is His way, His plan. I don't get it, but I don't have to. He's in charge!

If I were God, and having a clear understanding of man's reputation, I wouldn't have done it. No way!

IN OUR HANDS

For clarity let me reiterate, God can work independent of man and certainly has the authority to do so. Yet, He has chosen to work through us, in conjunction with us, His Church-that is you and me. None of us are perfect. Humans are flawed in many ways. We are frail and prone to failure. And yet, knowing all our deficiencies, He still placed and "entrusted" His message to our care.

Think about what God has done. The disbursement of the message of Jesus is entirely and solely in our hands.

16

Fascinating.

Since the above is true, we must take an inventory of our reality. The hour is late and the days are rapidly coming to a close. Collectively, we stand at a unique time in history. The stakes have never been higher.

We are the closers. No longer can we just look to God to "do it all." Idleness and lack of participation are no longer an option.

As you read this chapter billions upon billions of people all over the globe are desperately waiting to hear from His Church, His followers, His witnesses. They are sitting on the cusp of eternity completely unprepared to meet God—one heartbeat from eternal darkness. We must answer these questions honestly: Where are the laborers? Where are the messengers? Where is the Church? What are we doing with this great responsibility?

I have zero doubt that we are the generation that will usher in the return of Christ. May we not miss the opportunity to take our place in history and do what no other generation has been able to do: finish the job!

We must aggressively embrace the challenge, accept what has been *entrusted, given,* and *committed* to us, and finish well. The heavenly host is watching and the world is waiting. We have been created for this moment.

Andrew Jackson the seventh president of the United States, said it best. "I've got big shoes to fill. This is my chance to do something. I have to seize the moment."

In the chapters that follow, I will explore the significance of Jesus placing the care of the gospel into our hands in conjunction with

His "sitting down." It will be a journey that will leave a mark on you.

Let's seize the moment!

Prepare to be changed. Prepare to stand up.

2.

Moving Day

I hate moving, don't you? Surely moving has to be one of the punishments for the occupants of hell. There is no room for debate, moving is one of the worst possible things a human has to do. I despise it!

Prior to a move my wife and I like to have a huge garage sale. If we don't sell it, we will give it away, so we don't have to box it, carry it, load it, carry it again, unbox it, and finally put it in a permanent place. Did I mention I *loathe* moving?

On one of our moving days, I made a colossal mistake. Mind you, it was an honest mistake, but a mistake I will never make again.

When I scheduled a guest speaker to address our men's ministry I had no idea that the date of the meeting and our moving day would collide. Well they did, big time. To make up for my blunder, I came up with a brilliant plan; I would hire a two man moving team to move us. Then after a couple of hours, as soon as the meeting was over, I would hurry home to help finish things. Sounds reasonable, doesn't it? I thought this was a perfect plan. Mistake number one.

After carefully explaining to Karen the dreadful conflict and my masterful remedy, she gave me the go-ahead to attend the men's meeting rather than my helping with the move. Astonished and a little surprised by her calm response, I walked away relieved to have her approval. Mistake number two.

Later, after rethinking my intended course of action and pondering and analyzing my wife's low-keyed response I came to the conclusion that things are not always what they seem. I wisely determined going to the men's meeting may not be the healthiest and most prudent thing for me. So, after a few minutes of self-reflection and a personalized pep-talk, I humbly and softly re-approached her and offered to miss the meeting to stay and help with the move. Again, to my surprise, she insisted that I go. With no hesitation and without taking the time to deliberate, brainlessly I said, "Okay!" Mistake number three. Do you see a trend here?

Needless to say, in a very brief span of time, I broke numerous basic fundamental laws of how to make and keep a happy marriage.

Truthfully, I think my quick, not well thought out un-remorseful and overly happy, "Okay!" sent her over the edge.

One of the things men know subconsciously about marriage (it's like you are born with this secret knowledge), is that you never want to get your wife close to the "edge." The edge of *disappointment, frustration, unmet expectations,* and downright *disgust.*

I have learned the hard way that just the sight or even the smell of the edge can on many levels be disastrous for the

I got the "look" - you know the "hollow-death-stare."

husband. Not trying to be offensive but every married man knows what I am saying.

Furthermore, as I have painfully discovered on multiple occasions, the ongoing and troubling challenge for men is that the edge "moves" from day to day. It shifts. While you sleep, it travels. When you are at work, it is in transit. It's unfair. The edge is ever evolving and can just show up without warning anywhere and at any time. It is in continuous motion. For example, you can be at dinner having a perfect conversation and then "BAM!" It happens. Right there in the middle of the restaurant, the "edge" appears out of nowhere. Before you know it and have a chance to talk her away from the edge, she leaps. At that point its game over and it can take days and sometimes weeks for things to get back to normal.

Well, on that day I definitely found the edge. It abruptly appeared when I hastily said one simple, innocent word, "Okay!"

I pushed her so far over the edge there was no getting her back. How did I know this? I got *"the look"* - you know the "hollow-death-stare." I was horrified. I feared for my life. She appeared to have no soul. To this day I still shiver just thinking about it. Her cold expression is forever seared into my mind. To make things worse, immediately following the "look" I also got the *"silent"* treatment. This two-pronged response came all at once in one package. I knew I was doomed. Lights out. There was nothing I could do.

In mere seconds, right before my eyes, it seemed as if I was watching a horror movie. Her ears became pointed; fangs protruded out of her mouth; horns grew from her head. Her blues eyes turned hideously dark, her tongue forked, and in the blink of an eye, her fingernails grew four inches. In a desperate attempt to survive the moment, I even whispered the name Jesus. But nothing changed. In my heart I cried for divine intervention; I needed God's help. I begged Him for mercy, but the heavens were closed, I got no response. Nothing. It was as if Jesus wanted to see how this would end up.

I knew I stepped over into a dark abyss from where few men return to tell about it. It's the place men go when they commit an insane, inconsiderate grievance against their wife. It's called "Stupidville." Yep, and on that day I was given the keys to the city, made the guest of honor and even named mayor for the day.

> ...her blues eyes turned hideously dark, her tongue forked, and in a blink of an eye, her fingernails grew four inches.

At that point, there was nothing I could do to repair the situation. My destiny was sealed. Lesson learned.

Did I mention that I detest moving?

JESUS MOVED, TOO

Did you know even Jesus had a "moving day?"

In chapter 16 of the book of Mark, Mark records "moving day" in the life of Jesus. When Jesus ascended back to heaven He permanently changed His residence from earth to heaven. His move back home was a pivotal time in human history. Never again would He live on this planet in His fleshly body. He would no longer call the earth His home. Here is how it unfolded.

As the sun rose in the East, it seemed to be another typical Galilean day, hot, humid, and for the most part, uneventful. The city was busy with children playing, the marketplace buzzing, and people going about their way.

It had been 40 days since Jesus' resurrection, and, as He had done many times before, He met with His disciples. Like the other assemblies, this particularly scheduled closed meeting didn't raise any concerns.

All appeared normal and quite routine, but on that particular day, Jesus' agenda was altogether different. You see, it was the 40th day and that was significant. According to God's calendar, the 40th day after His resurrection was *moving day*. He was packing up and leaving because His physical time and ministry on earth had come to a close.

Jesus appeared to the eleven disciples one final time as they sat at the table, v. 14. He spoke candidly and told the disciples clearly what He wanted them to do.

YOUR LAST WORDS MATTER

When someone leaves on an extended trip or when a friend or loved one dies, everyone wants to know, "Did he or she have any last words?" People's last words are important because they represent what is dear to their heart. They desperately want their loved ones and friends to embrace and understand their final instruction. It is a crucial time, not only for the one departing, but also for those who are fortunate enough to hear their last words.

Little did the disciples know that this would be the last time Jesus would address them while on earth.

IT STARTED WITH A REBUKE

*"Later He appeared to the eleven as they sat at the table; and **He rebuked their unbelief and hardness of heart**, because they did not believe those who had seen Him after He had risen."*
(Mark 16:14)

His first words were stern and cut like a knife. He graciously, but boldly, rebuked them for not believing the report that He had risen from the dead (Mark 16:14). Ouch!

Their lack of faith astonished Him. Remember, this was 40 days after His resurrection. Why did He choose to scold them again at that time? Jesus apparently wanted to reemphasize the importance of faith and the role it would have in their life, ministry, and in the Kingdom of God. He was reminding them that only faith and love would advance

> *The disciples were sitting and eating, listening to Jesus talk, within a split second, something unimaginable happened.*

His cause. Jesus knew, without faith, they would be powerless and thoroughly ineffective.

After this razor-sharp correction, Jesus commanded His disciples concerning their work of the Kingdom. He outlined it this way, "Be witnesses to Me, preach My gospel to the whole world, and make disciples. But first, don't go anywhere. Wait here in Jerusalem for the Promise I told you about." Straightforward. Prioritized. Concise. (Mark 16:13f; Matt. 28:19,20; Luke 24:49).

It is evident, from the account, every word Jesus spoke mattered. It was a cram session for the disciples, and words were at a premium. Jesus' no-nonsense approach emphasized that time was of the essence and every second and moment was sacred. He was intentionally preparing them for their new life ahead, a life without His physical presence with them all the time.

As Jesus talked to them about their new responsibilities, no one had any idea what was about to take place. The disciples were sitting and eating, listening to Jesus talk. Within a split second, something unimaginable happened. There was no warning, no countdown, no last second goodbyes, no final hugs. He miraculously began to *float*. His feet left the ground, and He lifted into the air (Mark 16:14-19).

Naturally astonished, the disciples watched with amazement as He continued to ascend into heaven (Acts 1:9). In just moments, He vanished completely out of their sight. Jesus' last day on earth was over, and He had *moved on.*

> "Now it came to pass, while He blessed them,
> that He was **PARTED** from them
> and carried up into heaven."
> Luke 24:51
> (emphasis added)

> "Jesus **ASCENDED** to the right hand of God."
> Mark 16:19
> (emphasis added)

It is here that the *physical* separation occurred. Jesus and His disciples "parted" ways.

Remarkable! From this moment forward He would no longer be with them in His flesh and bone body. He was GONE!

However, Jesus would not leave His disciples alone. In just a matter of days, He would send the Holy Spirit to fill and empower them for their new roles (John 14:16-18; Acts 2:1-4).

As with any move, things are never the same. New environments, experiences, and responsibilities all accompany any change of address. Both Jesus and His followers had new roles and responsibilities.

There was a shift in the Kingdom of God.

While Jesus lived on the earth, He did most of the ministering: teaching, healing, preaching. His ascension repositioned Him, adjusted His role and changed His ministry platform. His move altered the disciple's responsibilities as well. Now the disciples were thrust into a new realm of authority and dependence. Instead of Jesus doing it "all"... He would now work through His disciples.

His MOVE changed everything.

E-V-E-R-Y-T-H-I-N-G!!!

3.

He Sat Down

"He was received up into heaven, and sat down..."
(Mark 16:19)

Over the years we have heard numerous sermons, teachings, and messages surrounding Jesus' extraordinary ascension, but I have never heard a message on Jesus "sitting down."

Naturally and in all fairness, we must give reverential attention to the phrase "He ascended." In fact, the ascension of Jesus was and is necessary for our salvation and sanctification. But let us not miss what happened after He ascended, **"and He SAT DOWN."**

You may wonder why we should bother with those four simple words? You ask, "What is the big deal?" To which I candidly respond, "It is a big deal...it is EVERYTHING!" This one uncomplicated, often over-looked event, altered everything. In fact, Christianity is where it is today and does what it does because of this statement, "and HE SAT DOWN."

The Bible references two reasons why Jesus has taken a seat in heaven.

First, Jesus sat down because He had courageously completed His assignment and purpose on earth by offering His blood and life for the sin of the world.

JUST NOT GOOD ENOUGH

In the Old Testament the work of the Levitical priests was constant and repetitious. Their labor of making atonement for the sins of Israel was ongoing and never completed. Needless to say, these priests carried an enormous burden and responsibility. They literally conducted hundreds of sacrifices each day by offering the Lord God the blood of pigeons, goats, doves, and lambs. There was little to no rest for these committed men.

*"**Day after day** every priest stands and performs his religious duties; **again and again** he offers the same sacrifices, which can **never** take away sins."*
Hebrews 10:11
(emphasis added)

Did you catch that? *"Day after day,"* *"again and again,"* the priest stood to perform blood sacrifices to make atonement for the sins of man.

Why?

The blessing of the chosen sacrifices of these animals and their provisions was temporary. The payment was insufficient and the benefit was short-lived. Each day the sacrifices expired. Therefore, the priest's work was continuous.

Furthermore, the Bible explicitly says God was **not pleased** neither satisfied with this system. The sacrificial system was woefully inadequate to deal permanently with the problem of man's sin.

*"Previously saying, "Sacrifice and offering, burnt offerings, and offerings for sin You did not desire, **nor had pleasure in them**"*
Hebrews 10:8
(emphasis added)

*"And every priest stands ministering daily and offering repeatedly the same sacrifices, **which can never take away sins.**"*
Hebrews 10:11
(emphasis added)

*"For it is **not possible** that the blood of bulls and goats could **take away sins.**"*
Hebrews 10:4
(emphasis added)

As the above scriptures indicate, this Old Testament system was deficient on many fronts. Therefore, it was problematic. Not only did it need to be amended, it needed to be completely replaced.

The solution?

Jesus!

*"For God so loved the world that He gave His
only begotten Son, that whoever believes in
Him shall not perish but have everlasting life."*
John 3:16

Jesus' one offering, one sacrifice had and has the capacity and potency to deal forcefully with the sin of man and eternally placate the judgment of God. Jesus was and is the answer!

Our massive personal sin debt was totally paid in full by the blood and life of Jesus.

Take a deep breath, meditate on the magnitude of Jesus' act of obedience. His pure sacrificial death on the cross and subsequent resurrection have purchased the salvation of the entire world, all of humanity. Our massive personal sin debt was paid in full with Jesus' life. The believer now stands before God clean, guiltless, forgiven, justified, whole, new, and completely pardoned. That is the gospel, "the good news!"

Also, because Jesus' offering was perfect He never again has to die for the sins of the world. Never again is a priest needed to offer sacrifices for the sins of men. Jesus was the spotless Lamb who was led to the slaughter (Isaiah 53:7) and ultimately arose to become our GREAT High Priest.

*"Therefore, since we have a **great high priest** who has ascended into heaven, Jesus the Son of God, let us hold firmly to the faith we profess."*
Hebrews 4:14
(emphasis added)

THE VOICE FROM THE CROSS

If you recall, one of Jesus' final statements from the cross was, *"It is finished"* (John 19:30).

These three words, "It is finished" come from one Greek word, *tetelestai,* meaning "FINISHED."

In Jesus' time various people in everyday life employed the word tetelestai. For example, a servant would use this word when reporting to his or her master, "Finished. I have completed the work assigned to me" (see John 17:4).

Furthermore, *tetelestai* is in the perfect tense in the Greek language so the full context of the word means, "It is finished, it stands finished, and it always will be finished!"

When Jesus shouted this phrase from the cross, He was saying the same thing. "The work I was given to do is done, and it will forever be done. FINISHED! I have completed the job."

We must thoroughly grasp this truth. There was nothing left for Jesus to do. He completed His assignment. Jesus satisfied all the demands of the law, therefore, after His ascension, **He sat down.**

"When he had made purification of sins,
He sat down *at the right hand of the Majesty on high"*
Hebrews 1:3.
(emphasis added)

"But when this priest had offered for all time one sacrifice for sins,
He sat down *at the right hand of God..."*
Hebrews 10:12
(emphasis added)

"To him who overcomes I will grant to sit with Me on My throne,
*as I also overcame **and sat down** with My Father on His throne."*
Revelation 3:21
(emphasis added)

It is wonderful to know that Jesus' sacrifice and death were perfect and complete! No longer is it necessary to offer a sacrifice for sin. Jesus was the flawless and last sacrifice. Job well done.

Now, here is the **second reason Jesus sat down** and the central focus of this book. When Jesus "SAT DOWN," He sent the message to His disciples, "My physical, in-the-flesh, earthly ministry is over...the preaching, teaching, performing of miracles, laying hands on the sick and acts of compassion are complete. I am done. ***Now it is your turn to go to work.***"

Pause. Slow down a bit. Look at those words meticulously. Pay close attention to every word. *"I am done. Now it is your turn to go to work."*

As I mentioned earlier, in all of my years of ministry I have never heard anyone refer to this as being one of the reasons Jesus sat down. However, this concept is both logical and scripturally sound.

CUTTING THE GRASS

Let me explain it this way. Not too long ago our family lived in the country. Our yard was not the typical yard. Each week I had to cut approximately five acres of grass. It was a daunting task, especially in the hot, humid, southern summer heat. When I completed my portion of the yard work, I would walk into my house, grab something to drink, *sit down* and relax. My portion of the job was done. My two boys would then complete the yard work; it was their turn to go to work. They would weed-eat and edge the driveway. *They would finish the job.*

Even though Jesus has finished His work on earth and has taken a seat in heaven, His mission continues, and that mission is carried forth by His sons and daughters.

Remember, Jesus knew all along the day was coming when He would turn the physical earthly ministry over to His followers. He had but three short years to train, develop and get His team ready to continue His work. That is why He prayerfully hand-picked twelve men to be with Him (Luke 6:12-13).

I would walk into my house, grab something to drink, sit down and relax.

Jesus understood that no day could be wasted and every hour mattered. The Jewish calendar year consists of 360 days, so, for a thousand and eighty days, He carefully invested and whole-heartedly poured His life into this company of believers. He walked with them, ate with them and slept under the open sky alongside them. They grieved, cried, laughed and played as a group. They did everything together!

Jesus was intent on preparing them for the day when He would ascend to heaven and *sit down*.

What an adventure it must have been to be in that first group and walk with Jesus on a daily basis, to have the privilege to hear Him speak, to be able to look deep into His eyes and to feel His compassion. Imagine what it might have felt like to watch Him become angry, to see Him flip tables over in the temple. Wow! They even had the privilege of sharing an intimate moment as He openly wept at the tomb of His close friend, Lazarus.

> *Imagine what it might have felt like to watch Him get angry, to see him flip tables over in the temple.*

What would it have been like to hear Him pray, to be in a boat on the Sea of Galilee as He walked by, to watch and listen to Him laugh, or hear how He talked to and interacted with his mother? The first twelve got all of this and much more.

Every day was chocked full of wonderment. For example, with His disciples close by His side, Jesus confronted the misguided religious Zealots of the day. He aggressively challenged their hypocrisy and objected to their double standards. On more than one occasion Jesus made the religious hierarchy so angry that they wanted to kill Him and all His buddies. It became quite apparent to all that Jesus wasn't like the other rabbis. He was unique in every way.

His simple words often left the most prestigious, educated and politically astute baffled and confused. The authority and the manner in which He spoke opened the hearts of the humble, yet it befuddled the Pharisees and Saduccees. The practicality of His profound wisdom amazed even His most hardened adversaries.

In all situations, Jesus exemplified to His disciples how to honor God and love people. For instance, when they witnessed Jesus touching the lepers, He did the unthinkable. Time and time again He modeled what it meant to love the unlovable and to care for society's outcasts.

Furthermore, the disciples regularly saw forgiveness and mercy on full display. While some picked up rocks to stone the woman caught in the very act of adultery, He drew in the sand. He forgave her and compassionately said, *"Go and sin no more."*

Also, He taught His friends how to talk to God and pray with effectiveness. He stressed the importance of having a vibrant love relationship with the Father. He emphasized time and time again that this relationship cannot and should not be about keeping empty rituals, abiding by rules and regulations. He modeled simplistic communion with the Father. This idea and example were foreign to them.

They had never heard or seen anyone like Him. He was different, completely otherworldly. He was God in the flesh.

More than once the disciples watched as life reentered dead bodies, i.e., the son of the Widow of Nain (Luke 7:11-17), and Jairus' daughter (Mark 5:22-43). They accompanied Jesus to Lazarus' tomb. Dead four days, the odor of decaying, rotting flesh was undeniable. Themselves in anguish over the loss of their friend, absorbing the scene and sounds. Seconds later, astounded, they witnessed Lazarus emerge in resurrection power full of life, as a result of Jesus speaking three simple words, *"Lazarus, come forth!"*

While they journeyed with Him, they observed remarkable miracles. The healing of blinded eyes, the opening of deaf ears. They watched, startled, as He walked on water, stunned as He calmed a violent sea. They were in awe as He took some pieces of bread and a couple of fish and feed nearly 20,000 people. They experienced what the prophets of old only dreamt of, God's glory on full display.

The disciples were amazed at His authority. His tenderness was unsurpassed and even infectious. Each day He demonstrated unfettered grace and love. He was God among them. Unequaled in power.

Needless to say, at every level Jesus' teachings challenged the disciples. At times they didn't understand His parables and even on occasion questioned His purpose. Much was required of them. In the midst of it all, He pressed upon them the importance of abandoning all to follow Him (Luke 9:23-26).

When Jesus chose His inner circle of disciples, He knew His assignment on earth was a temporary engagement. With each new sunrise, Jesus realized the day was fast approaching when He would rely on His disciples to continue His cause. However, His disciples did not know this.

Therefore, during the three difficult years of Jesus' ministry, He continuously poured the entirety of Himself into His beloved followers. Often, Jesus would neglect or withdraw from the larger crowd to spend valuable quality time with His disciples. In doing so, He specifically and intentionally prepared His followers to continue His work and, unbeknownst to them, strengthened them for His eventual departure.

> *He carried the weight knowing all but one of His friends would lose their lives because of Him.*

The New Testament makes it clear that Jesus loved His disciples immensely and cherished their relationship (John 17:6-26). Sadly, Jesus also understood, in mere days, after His resurrection, He would thrust His beloved friends into the heart of a raging battle, a spiritual war involving two worlds. He knew it would not be easy for them, and they would be called upon to make great sacrifices. Deep down, He carried the weight knowing all but one of His friends, John, would lose their lives because of Him. Therefore, He labored endlessly preparing them for the combat and challenges ahead.

THE SPEECH

Every athlete knows what it is like to receive a "pep" talk from the coach right before you take the field. The locker room is still, there is silence, and everyone listens to "the speech." The coach is giving his last set of directives and telling the team what it's going to take to win. It truly is a great moment.

In the last minutes of Jesus' life on this planet He gave a resounding talk to the team, His disciples, It is called the The Great Commission. Jesus discussed how the Church would spread the gospel. He outlined the new role the disciples were to have in the work of the Kingdom of God. It was His "locker room" speech, His game plan.

Interestingly, the word "commission" according to the Merriam-Webster Dictionary means: *"authority to act for, on behalf of, or in place of another."*

As He spoke His final words to His disciples Jesus was "commissioning" them to go in His place and with great authority, act, do, perform and speak on His behalf.

> *The body of Christ must grasp the severity of this truth: Jesus' physical in the flesh work on the earth is over. He completed His assignment.*

In essence, He looked at His disciples and said to them, *"Now it's your turn to go to work. Go and do what I did. Finish the job!"*

Jesus was preparing to sit down.

LET'S DO WORK

The body of Christ must grasp the severity of this truth: Jesus' ministry and work on the earth is over. He completed His assignment.

The very same assignment He gave to the twelve He now also gives to us. He has transferred the full weight and responsibility of that mandate to you and me, all of it. His job is now our job. We are His body, His hands, His voice, His hope. His touch. Without us, the world perishes.

The Church must also acknowledge that Jesus isn't going to get up and return to earth to do ministry. He isn't coming back to do our work, our portion for us. Remember, He sat down!

The great late W.A. Criswell who pastored First Baptist Church of Dallas for 46 years said it this way,

"There are no hands to do His work but our hands; no tongues to speak His testimony but our tongues; no life and shoulders strong and broad, and no dedication to build His kingdom in the hearts of men, but ours. And without our prayers and support and commitment, the church dies, and the mission dies, and the witness dies, and the testimony dies, and God's kingdom in the hearts of men dies."

At this very instant, Jesus is looking for His Church to finish what He started. It's our shift. It's our time to show up; it's time to punch the clock, pick up our tools and go to work. God needs us.

He has taken a seat. Will you stand up?

4.

Super Heroes

"With great power comes great responsibility."
Peter Parker, Spiderman

Who is it? Come on…tell me. Who is your favorite Super Hero? Spiderman, Incredible Hulk, Wonder Woman, Superman, Luke Skywalker, Wonder Dog, Iron Man, Mr. Incredible, Thor, Wolverine, Batman, Flash, etc.?

We all have one. Which one do you like the most? Did yours make the list?

Mine? Well, I have two equally favorites, Superman and Batman! I love those guys! Even to this day I get amped when I see their images or hear their intro music and lyrics. "It's a bird! It's a plane!

It's SUPERMAN!" Or, when I see those iconic words, "KAPOW!" "BAM!" "SPLAT!" explode on the screen as Batman and Robin lower the "BOOM" on those sinister villains. You add some chocolate chip cookies and milk...well, life doesn't get much better than that.

Everybody loves Super Heroes. The question is why? Among the many reasons is that Super Heroes *fix things*. They take wrong things and make them right. With their presence, the world becomes a safer place to live. We like that. Plus, it never fails, super heroes seem always to arrive on the scene at the climax of catastrophe and save the day just in the knick of time. Yes! In nearly every super hero story, movie and comic book the outcome is the same - the good guys win. We have grown to expect it. Isn't that what super heroes do?

IS GOD A SUPER HERO?

I am concerned that the majority of people view God the same way they do super heroes. We expect God to *fix things*, make things right, and slide in at the last moment to save the day regardless of our actions or behavior. Our conclusion, since God is *super powerful, almighty, loving* and *unequaled in His abilities,* He will automatically assert His strength and desire in every circumstance. Besides, isn't that what a God is supposed to do, especially one who is unmatched in His capabilities?

Super Heroes fix things.

Over the last few years I have observed that an overwhelming number of Christians are embracing a dangerous pattern of thought.

Before I reveal the unfortunate mindset, let me share with you the two devastating results it has had on the body of Christ.

First, it has led the church to have a misguided understanding of the current, right now, ministry of Jesus. For the most part, people don't grasp what Jesus, through His Church, His body, desires to do in the world and how He wants to do it.

Second, this distorted perspective has significantly contributed to a lack of involvement and engagement by many in the body of Christ. People have disconnected and generally do not see a need to participate personally in the efforts of the Kingdom of God.

With the above in mind, here is the new belief system that is having a catastrophic impact on our culture and world:

"No matter what we do or don't do, God's will on the earth will be done."

Interpretation: since God is in charge and controls all things He will see to it that His will is accomplished regardless of our actions or inaction.

This mindset embraces the following: because He is God, nothing happens or doesn't happen unless He wills it, both good and bad; therefore, no need to worry, all is well.

On the surface this sounds right, looks right and even appears to be theologically correct. However, this logic is flawed on two fronts.

One, this logic simply doesn't have biblical support. For example, bad things happened in the Bible that God never intended: David and Bathsheba, Israelites circling the wilderness for 40 years, Lot's wife becoming salt, etc.

Second, it does not stand up against the test of past and current realities.

REMOVAL OF GOD FROM SOCIETY

Let me give you some modern examples that will help you understand why "everything" that happens in the world is "not" God's will nor has His "approval."

Do you believe it was God's will to take prayer out of schools in 1963? No.

How about the removal of the "Ten Commandments" from schools and public buildings? No.

No one would deny that these two events alone have had a destructive and horrific impact on people's lives as well as our entire society.

These events were not God's will, but they still took place.

There is more.

Roe vs. Wade, in 1973, by a 7-2 vote, the Supreme Court made abortion legal in the United States. This decision legalized the slaughter of innocent babies in the mother's womb. God's will?

Again, no! Has everything worked out according to God's wishes as a result? No!

Here are the facts. Since 1973, based on data from both the Centers for Disease Control and the pro-abortion Guttmacher Institute, there have been over 50,000,000 babies that have lost their lives, violently murdered in their mother's womb. [2]

> *50,000,000 babies have lost their lives, violently murdered in their mother's womb.*

Sadly, each precious baby was in the process of being *"wonderfully made and fashioned"* by God Himself (Psalm 139:14). However, in the midst of God forming them they were killed mercilessly, their life snuffed out before their first breath.

Killing defenseless children was not nor will it ever be God's will. Period. But it happened despite God being against it. Sadly, over 3,000 babies a day are terminated.[3]

The examples above are just a small sampling of things that have occurred in our world that God neither intended nor desired. In fact, these decisions took place in spite of God's will, not because of God's will.

---

[2] Ertelt, Steven. "55,772,015 Abortions in America Since Roe v. Wade in 1973." Lifenews.com. http://www.lifenews.com/2013/01/18/55772015-abortions-in-america-since-roe-vs-wade-in-1973/.

[3] Life Matters TV Program. "LMTV Abortion Counter Background." LifeMattersTV.org. http://www.lifematterstv.org/abortioncounters.html.

This leads us to some important questions:

"If God did not want or will any of the above decisions and actions to take place, why did they?"

"Why didn't God invoke His will in these matters?"

"Why didn't God do the "super hero" thing and enforce His will and save the day?"

Here is my response to these questions.

First, God allows people, governments, and nations to make their own decisions.

Humans are not robots; we are free moral agents. God is not responsible for every decision that man makes. Nor is He responsible for the outcome of those decisions. Every person and nation has a will, and they make their choices based upon what they deem to be best for them. Some decisions are morally sound while others, regretfully, are not. When a person chooses to live their life without God they will choose a path that seems correct in their own eyes, but ultimately, in the end, it leads to death (Proverbs 16:25). And along the way their decisions impact the lives of others.

> *God has organized the world in such a way that He depends on us, His people, to work, do, and speak on His behalf.*

Here is my second response to the general question, "Why didn't God exert His power to stop these horrible decisions and actions?"

God has organized the world in such a way that He depends on us, His people, to work, do, and speak on His behalf. The Church is God's Ambassador and it is up to us to execute His will on earth, to be light in a dark world. Jesus taught His disciples to pray this very thing, "Your Kingdom come, your will be done on earth as it is in heaven (Matthew 6:10). Tragically, if God's people are apprehensive, complacent, silent and sedentary His purposes and plans can and will go unfulfilled, His commission will go unrealized. An undesirable consequence will follow-evil-and all that accompanies it, flourishes.

WHERE IS GOD?

The body of Christ must grasp the reality that God rarely intervenes and disrupts the outcome of His law of sowing and reaping (Galatians 6:8). In the extraordinary situation when He does, it is called a "miracle." However, the consensus state of mind in the Church is that God, somehow and somewhere along the way or in the end, will override the actions and desires of the people and no matter what we do or don't do God's will will come to pass. History and the Bible validate that this mindset is not truth. To believe this is both erroneous and dangerous.

> ...God's will-will be achieved no matter what we do or don't do.

Let me again explain by expounding on what happened in the 1960's. Not only was our nation facing immense cultural challenges, the Church was as well. Looking back through the lens of history, we now know the Church was unprepared to address the issues confronting the society it was supposed to impact. I don't want to come across as being harsh or judgmental, but my assessment is that the moral collapse we are now seeing in our society, generally, is a direct result of the seeds sown by sleepy church leaders plus the inactivity of the local churches and their members in that day. This current generation is reaping the harvest of a disinterested, frail, and disconnected church.

> *This current generation is reaping the harvest of a disinterested, frail, and disconnected church.*

For the most part, the Church has quietly watched from the sidelines trusting and hoping God's plan will come to pass. It hasn't.

> *For the most part, the Church has quietly watched from the sidelines trusting and hoping God's plan will come to pass. It hasn't.*

Sadly, some even accepted the outcome "as God's will" because according to their logic, "nothing happens" unless God "allows" it or "wills" it to happen.

TALKING POINTS OF A SLEEPING CHURCH

Have you noticed how we, the Church, have adopted cute one-liners and pious phrases to help us cope with the terrible state of affairs we are now facing? These slogans, while sounding biblical, allow us with a clear conscience to accept our prevailing moral collapse and all that comes with it by shifting the responsibility from us to God.

Here is a brief sampling of those dangerous, worn-out talking points of a napping Church.

"Nothing happens unless God allows it."

"It doesn't matter. God will work it out."

"God is in charge of everything."

"It's all going according to His plan."

"Everything happens for a reason…"

"If it happened God must have wanted it to happen."

These unchallenged mindsets have released in our generation and our churches an unprecedented level of confusion, indifference, disengagement, and apathy. This line of reasoning and approach to life has to stop.

The fact is, God works *through* us and when we don't work, His voice and influence is limited and evil prevails. If we don't do our part, His will is hampered, if not suppressed altogether. The

51

Church has been deceived and has become a spectator rather than a participator in the workings of God. Thus, we have a false sense of accomplishment and security.

YOU CAN'T DENY THIS

Before you stone me, let's take a rational look at what I'm saying. According to 2 Peter 3:9, God doesn't want one soul to be eternally separated from Him. However, all over the world, people are dying every day without responding to the message of Jesus, stepping into a Christ-less eternity. To make matters even worse, a significant portion of those perishing have never heard a clear presentation of the gospel.

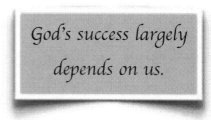

God's success largely depends on us.

At this moment the world population is 7.4 billion people. It is estimated 31%, 2.3 billion people, are adherents of Christianity. If true, this leaves an alarming 69%, 5.1 billion individuals who are not Christians.[4]

Furthermore, 42.2% of the world lives in what missiologists call an unreached people group.[5] An unreached people group is an ethnic group *without* an indigenous, self-propagating Christian church movement. Any ethnic or ethnolinguistic nation without enough Christians to evangelize the rest of the nation is an "unreached

---

[4] Pew Research Center. "The Future of World Religions: Population Growth Projections, 2010-20150." Pewforum.org. https://pewforum.org/2015/04/02/christians/.

[5] Joshua Project. "Global Statistics." JoshuaProject.net. https://joshuaproject.net/global_statistics.

people group".[6] Those that live in an unreached area have very little chance to hear the gospel in their lifetime.

To emphasize the magnitude and significance of these numbers, on average 55,300,000 people die annually.[7] If we keep true to the statistics then 31% of those who died are Christians and 17,143,000 individuals went to be with Jesus at their death. On the other hand, if 69% of those that died were unsaved then 38,157,000 stepped into eternity unprepared to meet God.

The most troubling part is that 42.2% of the 55,300,000 who died lived in an unreached people group. Therefore, 23,336,600 souls entered into eternity without hearing the gospel.

It looks like this:

151,506 people die each day.

If 31% of those who die daily are Christian, 46,966 go to heaven.

If 69% are not Christian, 104,539 experience the reality of hell.

If 42.2% live in an unreached people group, 64,000 people stepped into a Christ-less eternity without ever hearing the name of Jesus.

64,000!

How tragic! 64,000 precious souls that Jesus died for lived their entire life without hearing a clear presentation of the gospel.

---

[6] Wikipedia. "Unreached People Group." Wikipedia.com. https:// en.wikipedia.org/wiki/Unreached_people_group.

[7] Ecology. "World Birth and Death Rates." Ecology.com. http:// www.ecology.com/birth-death-rates/.

The numbers above are startling. How can this be still happening? Jesus gave the "Great Commission" to the Church 2,000 years ago and yet 42.2% of the world has virtually no chance to know about Him. No opportunity to embrace the Savior of the world. And tomorrow when we wake up, another 64,000 will perish for all eternity.

This is not God's will!

People are living and dying without hope, not because God is failing to do His job or that He wills people to perish in eternal darkness. May we not forget, Jesus wants all men to be saved; He has paid the ultimate price for their salvation. The truth is we are not doing our part. We are not obeying the call to go, witness and preach to the world. So, God's activity and "effectiveness" is limited and significantly impacted by our *inactivity, indifference, and disobedience*. I know this sounds extreme, but God's success largely depends on us. Again, both the Holy Scriptures and history witness to this truth.

ANOTHER EXAMPLE

Let me continue to make my case. All of us have seen the horrific pictures of starving children dying, their bloated bellies, hollowed-out eyes, their helpless limp bodies. The UNITED NATIONS recently reported on average 18,000 children die every day due to hunger and malnutrition.[8]

---

[8] USA Today. "18,000 Children Die Every Day of Hunger, U.N. Says." USAtoday.com. http://usatoday30.usatoday.com/news/world/2007-02-17-un-hunger_x.htm.

18,000!

Don't let that number fly through your thoughts without stopping and understanding the significance of such a gross total. Let me break it down for you. It is equivalent to 60 jumbo jets filled with passengers falling out of the sky every day. Let me say that again…60 jets. Unbelievable.

Each year, 6.5 million children lose their lives because of lack of food. Every hour 750 precious children die. Every minute 12 of those starving kids perish. Every five seconds a young life is gone. I am confident that not a single person would say this tragedy is the will of God. Children starving to death IS NOT His will, ever. Yet, this gruesome loss happens around the clock with no end in sight.

No one will ever be able to convince me that God willed or *approved* for these precious children to die at such an early age.

We live in a fallen world and horrid things do take place that God does not want to happen. Things that are not His will.

Who is responsible? Who gets the blame?

The fact is, many times when starving children die, when natural disasters take large swaths of life, and innocents are tragically killed in war, or for the most part, when bad things happen, the church immediately goes to its "talking points." While we have our "out phrases," "cute comebacks" and our "well thought-out and articulated rebuttals," the rest of the world points their finger at God.

We have all heard the questions from atheists, skeptics, and unbelievers, *"Where is your God? Why doesn't He intervene?"* or *"If God is God, all powerful and cares for people, why doesn't He do something to help these innocent kids?"* *"How can a God of love allow this to happen?"*

All of us have heard questions similar to these. What is your response? Do you have a clear, rational biblical answer? How do you defend God?

HE DOESN'T and to make matters worse, HE WON'T!

If we are honest we cannot deny that many in our society refuse to embrace Christianity and Christ based solely on these indictments. While we are huddled up in our cathedrals, the culture wants to know, and rightly so, "Where is God?"

To me, these are legitimate questions that should be asked and honesty answered.

Could God do something about the mass of hopeless souls stepping out into eternity each day? Could He intervene and stop the suffering and pain? Does God have the power and authority to cause food to fall from the sky and clean drinking water to shoot forth from the ground? Could He, with one snap of His finger, eradicate this terrible, gruesome cycle of death? The answer is emphatically, "yes, Yes, YES, He could." However, HE DOESN'T and to make matters worse, HE WON'T!

WHY?

Warning: the answer ~~may~~ will disturb you.

56

It is NOT HIS JOB ANYMORE!!!

He will not intervene. It is no longer *HIS* sole responsibility.

Take a deep breath. Relax. Think through the statements above before you walk away.

Don't forget, in the beginning, after creating Adam and Eve, God gave man jurisdiction and dominion over the earth (Genesis 1:26, 28). You may be wondering what that actually means? In short, mankind, who was created in His likeness, was and even to this day, is given care and oversight of the earth. Therefore, God's intervention into our world mainly comes through His children. We are the executors of His wishes and plans, conduits if you will. God chooses to operate through His people.

Also, if you recall, before Jesus ascended to heaven there was a great transfer of responsibility. He gave us, all Christians, His authority. He promised to be with us. And He delegated to each believer the task for executing His will and representing Him to the people of the world (Matthew 6:9,10). It is clear we are now His voice, His body (1 Corinthians 12:27), His extension of goodness, care, compassion, and love. God depends on each of us to do our part. In fact, this is what He expects us to do.

Our world is facing unprecedented calamity and devastation. And people everywhere want to blame God for all of the carnage that has taken place. But they fail to realize that God is more than willing to eliminate the heartache and suffering of our world. He loves people and takes no delight in their misery. He desires to demonstrate His tender compassion and unsurpassed power to hurting people. Right now, God is looking for willing vessels to work through (2 Chronicles 16:9).

People cannot ignore the fact that if we, His children, are unwilling or somehow do not cooperate with His plans then God's purposes go unfulfilled. Yes, *even* the things that are His will. Did you catch that? His will *does not* and *will not* happen.

In essence, if we fail to do what He instructs us to do then His will on earth doesn't get done. Kids don't get fed. Souls don't get saved. Period. No exceptions.

IT IS ALL PREVENTABLE

Again, the calamities mentioned above, children starving to death and vast amounts of people stepping into a Christ-less eternity could be prevented. How? By each member of the body of Christ unconditionally yielding their body, accepting their role, fulfilling their responsibility and simply doing what Jesus instructed us to do.

Unfortunately, the majority of believers haven't taken that step of involvement. For the most part, people have decided to play it safe. People have made the decision to sit back and look expectantly to God, our self-imposed Super Hero, to intervene and fix everything, make things right, and save the day.

This approach and mindset has resulted in the pernicious expansion of deep darkness and pain. We cannot allow this to continue. The hope of the world is God's power working through His children.

It's time to stand up.

5.

Orders

---

*"One day your life will flash before your eyes.
Make sure it is worth watching."*
Gerard Way

I had a great time growing up. My parents were amazing, and they created a wholesome, healthy home environment. We laughed a lot and truly loved each other. As a kid, I had so much fun running the streets of our neighborhood. Life was good, really good!

I vividly remember as a small child, my friends and I would play "Army." We would choose teams, build forts and run around the woods and play for hours. We used sticks for our guns and pine combs were our grenades. We would make the sound of the gun firing - "bang, bang, bang" - and then argue over who shot who first.

"I shot you."

"No, you didn't! I shot you!"

"Uh, uh, I shot you, you're dead!"

"No, I'm not, you're dead!"

Sometimes the argument over who shot who first would actually end up in an real fight. It was great fun!

OUR MILITARY

Like you, I have the utmost respect for the men and women who serve in the military. Soldiers, airmen, sailors, and marines voluntarily place their lives in harm's way to defend our freedoms so we can live in peace. They are special people and deserve our highest admiration at all times.

My father faithfully served in the Navy and I have other family members who have and are currently in the armed forces.

I have watched my nephews be commissioned and sent to spend extended periods of time on foreign soil and open waters. The days, weeks and months away from their loved ones and friends are tough. The sacrifices the men and women in uniform make for our country is enormous.

THESE WORDS MEAN SOMETHING

I recently discovered that when one enlists in the United States Military, active duty or reserve, they take the following oath:

"I do solemnly swear (or affirm) that I will support and defend the Constitution of the United States against all enemies, foreign and domestic; that I will bear true faith and allegiance to the same; and that I will obey the orders of the President of the United States and the orders of the officers appointed over me, according to regulations and the Uniform Code of Military Justice."

No wonder the United States has the world's finest, most disciplined, and strongest military in the world. The men and women who serve in the armed forces of this country understand and aggressively adhere to this oath, even if it costs them their life. This vow is not just empty rhetoric; it becomes their lifestyle and purpose.

Pay close attention to their duty, *"I solemnly swear... I will support and defend... I will obey the orders of the President... and the orders of the officers appointed over me...."*

Without question, a military's effectiveness and stability are built on the foundation of obedience to orders. As soon as a young recruit arrives for boot camp, they are taught to obey the orders of their superiors without hesitancy. A soldier who does not learn to follow orders jeopardizes the mission at hand and places not only his life but also the lives of those around him in peril.

> *...if a soldier disobeys an order during a time of war, that soldier can be sentenced to death.*

The new recruit completely understands that if one fails to obey the lawful orders of their superiors, they will face consequences for

61

their decision. In fact, the Uniform Code of Military Justice makes it a crime to willfully disobey a superior commissioned officer. And, if a soldier disobeys an order during a time of war, that soldier can be sentenced to death.[9]

Imagine if the military did not have this high standard of conduct. Chaos and insubordination would reign and things would quickly escalate out of control. Before the recruit signs the papers to enlist they are incontrovertibly made aware of these expectations and the consequences of failing to obey orders.

It is evident the leaders of our military know our country's protection and quality of life depend on soldiers following orders.

When it comes to the success of the Church, God also knows it's global impact depends on His children "following orders."

MARCHING ORDERS

The context of the following passage infers that Jesus spent the days after His resurrection with the disciples clarifying their soon-to-be new responsibilities.

Acts 1:2, The New American Standard Bible,

> *"until the day when He was taken up to heaven,*
> *after He had by the Holy Spirit **given orders** to the*
> *apostles whom He had chosen.*
> (emphasis added)

---

[9] Powers, Rod. "Military Orders." Thebalance.com. http://usmilitary.about.com/cs/militarylaw1/a/obeyingorders.htm.

This verse is significant. Look at what Jesus did after the resurrection during this important 40-day period... *"He gave orders to the apostles"* (v. 2).

Isn't that interesting? Jesus gave orders.

Considering what we discovered about the military, this scripture sheds light on Jesus' expectations.

It is safe to say Jesus wasn't reteaching the principles of the Ten Commandments. These precious few days with His disciples were not church gatherings where they came together to have quaint Bible studies. No, these 40 days were intense, focused and purposed driven. He **gave orders**.

The dictionary defines an "order" as *an authoritative direction or instruction, command or mandate.*

What exactly does it mean that Jesus *"gave orders"*?

Let's take a deeper look at Acts 1:2. The Greek word "order" strongly emphasizes the idea of Jesus "charging" His disciples to accomplish a distinct assignment.

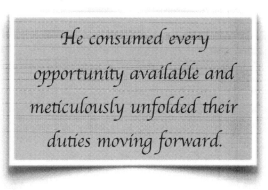

He consumed every opportunity available and meticulously unfolded their duties moving forward.

What Jesus did is similar to a military officer briefing and commissioning his soldiers before a deployment.

Remember, time is of the essence. Jesus is departing earth shortly, so He appoints and commissions His disciples for His purpose. Worth noting is that there were no miracles of healing recorded during this 40 day period. He exhausted every opportunity available and meticulously unfolded their duties moving forward. These precious few days were all about instruction, direction, teaching and assignment clarification. He gave them their marching orders.

This type of briefing and language wasn't completely foreign to the disciples. For example, in Luke 10, Jesus summoned his team and sent seventy of His followers out with specific orders to preach His message of hope, love, and power to the untapped harvest fields. It was a "trial run," a sign of things to come.

When the seventy returned from their mission, their hearts were filled with joy. The first thing they said was *"Lord, even the demons were subject to us in your name"* (v. 17). Don't miss that. The demons yielded to them! They were submissive to the "representative" of Christ. Because the disciples obeyed their leader in carrying out the mission assigned to them and exercised their authority in the name of Jesus, the demons had to yield to them.

Notice what Jesus said after their glowing testimonies, *"I saw Satan fall like lightning from the sky..."* (v. 18).

"MAY I HAVE YOUR ORDER?"

In our world, giving and taking orders is not new to us. Every day we see this in action. We are either giving orders or taking orders. For instance, when you walk into a restaurant to eat, you often see a sign that reads, "Place Order Here." Or when we sit at the table, the waitress walks up and says, "May I have your order." Perhaps at the drive-thru of a fast-food chain, a voice echoes, "Order when ready." Whatever you say to the attendant is an instruction, directive, or command. In other words, when you place an "order" with the server it his/her duty to make sure you receive all that you ordered. The quality of your experience at the restaurant is often impacted by how well and timely they fulfill your directive, or "order."

However, not all things work according to plan.

From time to time, all of us have seen the signs that appear on soda machines, water fountains, elevators, vending machines, coffee dispensers, gas pumps, etc.: **"Out of Order."** Don't you just cringe when you see it? They usually show up at the worst possible times.

If you are like me, you start asking yourself questions like:

"How long will it be out of order?"

"I wonder what's wrong with it?"

"Who broke it?"

"When are they going to fix it?"

Recently I was entering an airport loaded down with luggage. It seemed I had walked a mile to get to the terminal. The whole way I wrestled with two heavy suitcases and a carry-on bag. Finally, I made it; I was exhausted. I was looking  forward to catching my breath and enjoying the refreshing escalator ride up to the terminal. However, as I approached the escalator I saw a sign taped to an orange traffic cone that read, **"out of order."** I shouted to myself, "Out of order! No way!" I was beyond frustrated; I was mad! Why? I *needed* the escalator to work. I did not want to carry the 2,000 pounds of luggage up the stairs. I depended on the escalator to do what it was created to do, but it was "out of order." Yep, I needed it to be functioning properly to get me up to the terminal. Did I mention I "needed" it?

Needless to say it "not working" made life momentarily difficult. After a brief meltdown, I had to locate an alternate route to the terminal, the stairs. Why? The escalator was out of service. Inoperable. Inactive. "Out of Order."

So what does it mean when something is labeled "out of order?" It implies that it is not working properly or not working at all. In other words, it is not fulfilling its originally designed purpose, and not doing what it was built and commissioned to do. And when this happens someone sticks a sign on it, that reads "out of order."

ORDERS VS. SUGGESTIONS

Not once is the Great Commission ever referred to as the Great Suggestion. Too many Christians treat the orders He has given as recommendations, options to pursue if convenient. The Church cannot continue to operate with that mindset.

While we are forever thankful for the specificity of the Great Commission, His orders are not limited to it. They include multiple areas of our life such as holy living, sharing the gospel, prayer, discipleship, application of the Word of God, etc. Here is another example. God expects us to serve Him faithfully in the church we attend. Not just as a spectator or consumer but an active part of the army of God in that church. Unfortunately, statistics prove the vast majority of church goers do little to nothing in the way of service in their local church. Our involvement in our church must go beyond attending worship services. It has to be more than dropping a few dollars in the offering plate, showing up to sing a few songs and settling in to hear an inspiring message from the pastor. According to Romans 12:1, the aforementioned is our "reasonable service." The least of what we should be doing. We must do more.

A COMPLETE EXCHANGE OF PURPOSE

When one enlists in our nation's armed forces, he/she gives up control of their lives. The particular branch of the military they join now virtually dictates every movement - what they are to wear, where to live, where to go and what orders they must follow. As Christians, we have chosen to enlist in God's army and following God's orders has to become our highest priority. To disobey or not fulfill His wishes certainly should not be an option for us. The moment we become born again Christ becomes our General, our Commander-in-Chief, and our passion should and must be to please Him.

2 Timothy 2:3,

> *"You therefore must endure hardship as a*
> ***good soldier*** *of Jesus Christ. No one engaged in*
> *warfare entangles himself with the affairs of this life,*
> *that he may **please him** who enlisted him*
> *as a soldier."*
> (emphasis added)

THEIR ORDERS ARE NOW OUR ORDERS

As one reads the Scriptures, it becomes clear that He now gives us the same specific assignments and instructions that were given to the early disciples. Their responsibilities have become ours.

How are you doing with those "orders"? How engaged are you? Are you faithful? Are you reporting for duty at the church you attend?

Can the church leadership count on you to do your part?

Are you engaged in the fight?

How dependable are you?

Are you obeying the Father's orders?

> *When the Pastor sees you, what does he see? Does he see a sign taped to your chest that reads "out of order?"*

When the Pastor sees you, what does he see? Does he see you completely committed to the vision of the house? Are you "reporting for duty?" Or, when he looks at you does he see a sign taped to your chest that reads, "out of order?"

We cannot afford to misinterpret the time in which we live. Time is short. The days of passive commitment and indecision are over. Our inactive status must come to an end. We need every abled body to report for duty ready to fulfill the Master's orders. And when you stand before Him, may you hear, "Well done, good and faithful servant."

6.

The Christmas Scarf

It is truly a great moment when you open a gift from someone you love. Very few things in life rival the anticipation, the adrenalin rush, and the joy of that moment. Honestly, the unwrapping of a gift brings out the child in all of us; it is an extraordinarily special time. However, there is one exception: when you open a gift you have previously owned for years. Yep, this is my story.

69

I enjoy giving gifts to others, but I must confess, I am not the best at doing so. Recently at Christmas, my wife opened a gift from me that I meticulously, lovingly, and painstakingly wrapped. I was excited about the gift. However, there was this one itty-bitty problem. The gift I gave her was a scarf; not just any scarf, but a scarf she already owned and had worn often. That's right. In fact, she even wore this same scarf on the very day we went Christmas shopping as a family. Talk about being completely clueless and not paying attention to details.

What happened? Well, to the best of my knowledge, at some point while we were at the mall, she decided to remove her scarf and evidently placed it in the bag of gifts that I was carrying. Later that evening when the boys and I gathered to wrap her gifts, we collected all the items out of the bags. At first, I thought the scarf looked familiar. I held it, analyzed it, and even put it up to my nose to smell it. It smelled like her; it had the scent of her perfume. But it didn't register with me that this was her scarf. I even asked my grown boys, who were wrapping her gifts with me, if they recognized the scarf. Each emphatically said, "no." Indeed, "it" runs in the family. So, we confidently drew the conclusion that if it was in the bag, we must have bought it for her even though none of us recall purchasing it. We were so convinced that we didn't verify the purchase by looking at the receipts. Does the movie *Dumb and Dumber* come to your mind?

SIDE NOTE: With my being responsible for leading my children it is no small miracle the boys survived childhood. I believe in the supernatural.

CHRISTMAS ~~MOURNING~~ MORNING

So you guessed it. On Christmas morning she gladly ripped into the beautifully wrapped package and opened the gift, the scarf she had owned for years. Here is the amazing thing, to her credit she smiled, acted surprised, tried it on and graciously said, "I love it, it's beautiful, thanks." We were clueless and did not know that she knew all along that this was her scarf.

The boys and I smiled real big. We were happy and proud because we gave Karen a gift she loved - so we thought. However, on the inside, she had to be thinking, "I am surrounded by a bunch of unbelievable idiots." What a lady!

THE GIVER OF GIFTS

In the New Testament you discover Jesus gives special gifts to His children. The good news: they are not repackaged or previously "worn" gifts. These gifts are unique and particularly suited for each of us.

1 Peter 4:10,

*"As **each one** has **received a gift**, minister it to one another, as good stewards of the manifold grace of God."*
(emphasis added)

Ephesians 4:8 says,

"When He ascended on high,
He led captivity captive,
*And **gave gifts to men**."*
(emphasis added)

Here is what we know. According to the texts above, as Jesus was ascending to heaven, **before** He **sat down**, He "distributed" spiritual gifts to His followers.

"…and *gave gifts to men*."
(emphasis added)

Why before He sat down?

His earthly ministry was over so as He ascended, He dispersed individual gifts/tools/weaponry to His brand new army. He was giving them everything they needed and every possible advantage so they could carry out His orders (Matthew 28:19,20; Mark 16:14-20).

Notice the sequence. First, Jesus gave the disciples their **mandate** and **marching orders.** Then He gave them the **tools** necessary to accomplish His mission.

Both of these events occurred before He sat down.

GIFTED FOR WAR

Imagine, if you will, a General sending his soldiers to war without the necessary equipment to accomplish the important objective. It would be disastrous. Lives would be lost and resources wasted. They would call into serious question the competency of such a leader

He was giving them everything they needed and every possible advantage so they could carry out His orders.

and rightfully so. Jesus understood this, and He knew His followers would be incapable of carrying out His mission if they were not properly equipped and furnished with the necessary tools to get the job done, especially against an enemy like the devil who is resilient, shrewd, and cunning. Therefore, He gave spiritual gifts to His disciples so they could adequately carry out the mission of the Church.

Many people ask, "What is a spiritual gift?" A spiritual gift is a supernatural endowment or tool Jesus gives to each believer so the Christian can fulfill their unique mission for Christ in the local church and the world.

At this point, it is important to answer two questions: 1. What kinds of "gifts" were given; 2. To whom were these gifts given?

The answer is "spiritual gifts" and they are mentioned in 1 Corinthians 12; Romans 12; Ephesians 4.

Additionally, these gifts were given and are given to His children, believers, as it pleases Him.

Here are four facts every Christian needs to understand.

4 BASIC TRUTHS

1. EACH MEMBER OF THE BODY OF CHRIST HAS BEEN GIVEN A SPIRITUAL GIFT

The Bible teaches that the moment a person is converted, two things happen. First, you are placed into the body of Christ,

1 Corinthians 12:18. And secondly, a "spiritual gift" is deposited into your life (1 Peter 4:10). Worth noting, Romans 12:3-8 and 1 Corinthians 12:12-18 further validate that God distributes His gifts to His children and places us into the body as He desires.

2. NOT EVERYONE KNOWS THEY HAVE A SPIRITUAL GIFT

When people don't know they have a spiritual gift, the result is tragic and has far reaching repercussions. The fact is that on any given Sunday, our church buildings are packed with scores of Christians who have no idea they have been given a spiritual gift. They come to church and enjoy the surroundings, fellowship and partake in heartfelt worship. They leave blessed, encouraged, inspired and challenged by the experience. They

> *I am convinced that when pastors stand before God, He is not going to ask them the "how many attended your church" question.*

don't realize that God has endowed them with an extraordinary gift/tool to be used for His purposes. Therefore, their spiritual gift, which was divinely placed inside of them, lies idle for the most part, in a state of dormancy. Consequently, they are unable to be thoroughly used by the Lord. Other than "being saved" they make little to no contribution to the cause of Christ. Unfortunately, many of these Christians will live and die never realizing their Heavenly Father gave them a "spiritual gift."

3. CHURCH LEADERSHIP MUST HELP BELIEVERS DISCOVER THEIR GIFT

In simple terms, the role of church leadership is to help believers identify their spiritual gift. I am convinced that when pastors stand before God, He is not going to ask them the *"how many attended your church"* question. I do believe God will ask pastors what they did with the raw material He sent them. In other words, what did the pastors do with the recruits in their church? How did they develop and prepare them so He could get maximum output from them? Each church should have a systematic approach to help people who come to their church identify their gifting.

> Many churches and ministries focus mostly on building their attendance numbers and not so much on developing, training, and equipping an army that can penetrate deep within the gates of hell.

4. EQUIPPING PEOPLE TO USE THEIR GIFT MUST BE A TOP PRIORITY OF THE CHURCH LEADERSHIP

Many churches and ministries focus mostly on building their attendance numbers and not so much on developing, equipping and training an army that can penetrate deep within the gates of hell.

The focal point of Jesus' ministry was never about the "crowd." He was never impressed nor was He motivated to attract the masses.

His approach was different. He chose twelve men, trained and equipped them for spiritual advancement. He "made/molded" these men into a powerful physical and spiritual force. The priority of our churches must be the same. Paul understood this and it became His message to the church at Ephesus.

Ephesians 4:11-12,

> *"And He Himself gave some to be apostles, some prophets,*
> *some evangelists, and some pastors and teachers,*
> *12. for the **equipping** of the saints for the work of ministry,*
> *for the edifying of the body of Christ..."*
> (emphasis mine)

Don't miss what Paul said to church leaders: the ultimate responsibility of the church leadership is to equip the believers for God's use. In the original language, the word "equip" in verse 12 means, "complete furnishing, perfecting, a fitting or preparing fully." [10]

WHAT MUST WE DO?

Pastors, Church Leaders, the assignment is crystal clear, *"perfect/ equip the saints for the work of the ministry...."*

Paul doesn't mince words; he is emphatic. The responsibility of the five-fold ministry offices, "Apostle, Prophet, Pastor, Teacher, Evangelist," (Ephesians 4:11) is to make sure that the believers under their care are completely furnished and trained to do what

---

[10] Blue Letter Bible. "Strong's G2677 - *katartismos.*" https:// www.blueletterbible.org/lang/lexicon/lexicon.cfm?Strongs=G2677&t=KJV.

they have been gifted to do. God needs us to make sure His army is thoroughly prepared for service and battle. This is job number one.

- *the church is a modern day "outfitter"* -

If you have ever watched a hunting show or know someone who loves the outdoors you are probably familiar with the term "outfitter."

Whether a person is going on an exotic hunt out west, white water rafting on the Colorado River, or walking the Appalachian Trail, an outfitter has the responsibility to equip their client with the necessary clothing, tools, and resources for survival and to ensure maximum enjoyment of their chosen expedition.

The ultimate responsibility of church leadership is *"outfitting"* church members for the work of God. In essence, to make sure the believers under their care are properly trained and "fitted" for every situation. Their usefulness to the King must be the Church's highest goal.

WHY DON'T WE DO THIS?

The commitment to prepare God's people for service takes work and is not easy. Often the process can be disheartening, not to mention time-consuming. Discouragement is commonplace. These reasons alone are why most churches don't proceed effectively in their efforts to train their people for the work of the ministry. Regrettably, when churches and their leaders see minimal fruit they often go into default mode. Their attitude becomes: "Let's just have 'good church,' let God handle the details. God will fix them. He will work it all out."

> *Sadly, we have discovered people can come and enjoy our really cool worship services week after week and experience "good church" and yet never become profitable for Jesus.*

This approach and attitude have to change now. We have to take seriously this mandate to *"equip the saints for the work...."*

It is of utmost importance that today's believers become profitable to the Master. Sadly, we have discovered people can come and enjoy our really cool worship services week after week and experience "good church" and yet never become profitable for Jesus (Matthew 25:30). People have to be equipped and carefully trained to be useful to Him.

2 Timothy 2:21

> *"...and **useful** for the Master, **prepared** for every good work."*

Notice this word "prepared." It means, "to make something ready for use." Paul told Timothy, "Your usefulness to Jesus depends on how well you are prepared." Oh my! Leaders, here is our job description; this is what we must do. PREPARE OUR PEOPLE FOR THE MASTER'S USE!

This mandate has to consume us!

THE GOOD NEWS

A church that makes this the priority of their ministry will always be in a state of growth and increase. Here is the promise, God's word:

> *16 "from whom the whole body, **joined and knit together** by what every joint supplies, according to the effective working by which **every part does its share, causes growth** of the body for the edifying of itself in love."*
> Ephesians 4:16

When we methodically "perfect, equip and train" (Ephesians 4:12) our church members, Ephesians 4:16 is the expected result. The body, the church will grow. Right here is God's formula for building the local church, "Equip the saints…and let them do their share…" (Ephesians 4:12,16).

TOUGH QUESTIONS:

Do you know what your spiritual gift is? If so, how are you using this gift in your church for His glory? Who is training you on how to use this gift more wisely and more effectively.

In addition, what procedures and tools does your church employ that helps people discover their gift?

Also, if I came to your church and asked you, "How can I identify my spiritual gift?" what response would you have? Or, if I asked you, "Can you train me how to use this gift?" what action would you take? How would you proceed in "outfitting" me for Jesus' use?

Do you and your church have a plan?

Each church and leadership team must have a procedure that helps people discover their spiritual gift and an efficient system to train and equip them to use their gift.

This process is God's way, His plan! Let's do it His way.

7.

The Holy Ghost

The key is not money, organization, cleverness, or education.
Are you and I seeing the results Peter saw? Are we bringing
thousands of men and women to Christ the way he did? If not,
we need to get back to His power source..."
Jim Cymbala

Days earlier, at the Garden of Gethsemane, in the dark of night, the disciples fled and ran for cover after the soldiers arrested Jesus. Later that evening, the leader, Peter, supposedly their strongest, quickly cowered in the face of a young girl who accused him of being a follower of Christ. The Bible records, not just once, but three times he denied knowing the Master.

Surprisingly, the disciple's hasty withdrawal mixed with Peter's denial of Jesus disclosed to everyone that in their own strength, the

> *Their hearts were good; they were well intentioned, but that was not enough nor would it be.*

disciples would have no chance at all of continuing the work of Jesus.

Now, more than ever, this select group of followers was vulnerable, fragmented, fragile and weak. Their hearts were good; they were well intentioned, but that was not enough nor would it be.

Since the day He called them to join Him, He knew of their frailties. He recognized better than anyone they would need more, much more in order for them to be effective. They would need supernatural empowerment. The task ahead was too daunting for them to attempt it in their limited capacity.

For this reason, both publicly and privately, Jesus spoke often of the Holy Spirit. On many occasions, He purposely taught about the role the Spirit would have in their lives and ministry. He was strategically preparing them for the day they would receive and experience the power of the gift of the Holy Spirit.

UP TO THIS POINT

Before we proceed it is important to review two things Jesus did with and to His disciples after His resurrection.

FIRST: Before His ascension and during the 40 day period after His resurrection Jesus reminded the disciples of **their assignment and responsibility** (Matthew 28:19,20; Acts 1:2).

SECOND: As Jesus was ascending He **distributed spiritual gifts** to each of them so they could have the tools necessary to carry out His orders (1 Corinthians 12:18; 1 Peter 4:10; Ephesians 4:8).

These first two events now lead us perfectly to Jesus' next step.

THE THIRD ACTION: *The outpouring of the Holy Spirit.*

NOBODY LIKES TO WAIT!

"Behold, I send the Promise of My Father upon you;
*but **tarry in the city** of Jerusalem until you are*
endued with power from on high."
Luke 24:49

Before His ascension, Jesus charged this eager band of disciples with a cosmogonic mandate, *"Go into all the world and preach the gospel and make disciples"* (Matthew 28:19). However, before He released them with this global task He said, *"Wait, I don't want you to go until you have received power from heaven."*

He gets them all fired up and then says, "Wait. You can't go just yet."

Think about it. The disciples have spent 40 days with the Master listening to Him share His heart and love for the world. He meticulously discusses their new role and responsibilities. They reflect on all the miracles He performed. He promises to accompany them. He gets them all fired up and then says, *"Wait. You can't go just yet."*

I am sure they were more than a little puzzled. I can hear them now, "Wait for what? We are ready! We can do this! Jesus, You trained us. You showed us exactly what to do, release us now!"

Jesus was emphatic. His instructions could not have been clearer. They were not to do anything at all. Absolutely no ministering in any capacity, which included preaching, teaching, healing, or even making disciples. They were told to *tarry, not move,* and to *stay put* until they experienced the fullness of the Holy Spirit upon their lives (Luke 24:49; Acts 1:4).

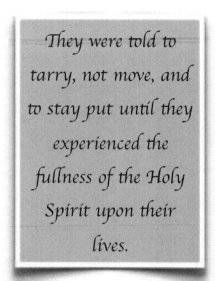

They were told to tarry, not move, and to stay put until they experienced the fullness of the Holy Spirit upon their lives.

Certainly, they were restless and anxious to begin this new chapter of their lives. They were privileged to walk with Jesus day in and day out. They had an eye-witness account of Him in action as He raised the dead, opened blinded eyes, and caused the lame to walk. Keep in mind He was crucified days earlier, and now He's alive standing in their very presence. Their confidence had to be high.

Furthermore, I am sure they also remembered what He said to them in John 14:12,

> *"...he who believes in Me, the works that I do he will do also; and greater works than these he will do...."*

They also knew He would never leave them alone,

"I am with you always..."
Matthew 28:20

Therefore, I completely understand their desire to go preach, teach and minister. There was an urgency to lead people to God and to help those who were hurting.

Nevertheless, the disciples were instructed to wait.

CHURCH PLANT #1

In spite of their soaring confidence and their eagerness to begin, I am sure the disciples were a little nervous. Who wouldn't be? Think about it. They were

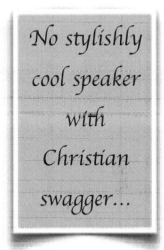

personally selected by Jesus to be on the launch team to start the first church ever. Talk about pressure!

Obviously, this wasn't your modern day typical church start. There would be no slick mass marketing blitz to garner the community's attention, no eye-catching logo, no hot band, no cool lights, zero hazers or movers, no HD environmental projection system, no social media to leverage the new beginning, no mantra promising, *"You will like our church cause we are different"* and certainly, no mocha latte served in the chic' cafe. And most astonishing, no stylishly cool communicator with Christian swagger or ultra fashionable worship leader. No, just a simple launch team of average men and women who quietly obeyed their leader's wishes, *"Stay. Don't do anything until you are endued with power."*

THEY NEEDED POWER!

Here is why Jesus gave the command to His disciples to tarry and to wait for the Holy Spirit: The Church's success and effectiveness hinged on them being "endued with power."

Jesus, better than anyone, understood that ministering in human effort alone would be woefully insufficient. He knew they would never be able to represent Him adequately and to defeat the opposing forces without His strength and power.

His followers needed power, not just any kind of power, His POWER! Resurrection power.

Luke 24:49,

> *"Behold, I send the Promise of My Father upon you;*
> *but tarry in the city of Jerusalem until you are*
> ***endued** with **power** from on high."*
> (emphasis added)

This scripture puts things into perspective. And to fully understand the volume of Jesus' command we must closely analyze the words "endued" and "power".

> *The Church's success and effectiveness hinged on them being "endued with power."*

First, lets take a look at the word power. The Greek noun used for power, in verse 49, is *dunamis*, from which we get our English words dynamo, dynamic, and dynamite. This alone ought to give you an indication of the purpose of the Holy Spirit. Also, according to Strong's Exhaustive

Concordance, *dunamis* should be interpreted as *force* or *miraculous power*.

The next word we want to review is the word *endued*. The Greek word used is the verb, *enduo*, which means to put clothing on or apparel on someone, to clothe, to be clothed or covered. It gives us the image of someone who puts on additional clothing or a coat before they step outside into the cold weather. They cover themselves.

Going to the Upper Room was not a request, but an order, a command.

Here is what Jesus was trying to communicate to His disciples, *"Do not go into the world and even attempt to represent Me until you are covered, clothed and dressed with My dynamic, explosive supernatural power, force, and ability, My Spirit."*

Whatever we do, we cannot miss the implication of Jesus' instruction. Notice, going to the Upper Room to wait for the outpouring of the Holy Spirit was not a request but an order, a command. He knew the *Holy Spirit* would give the disciples the capability, strength, and capacity to represent Him on the earth and to accomplish and fulfill His orders with supernatural power, force, and ability.

One has to assume if the outpouring of the Holy Spirit was necessary for the launch of the first church, how much more necessary is it for us today?

8.

The Baptism of the

Holy Spirit

"We have created a Christian market
instead of a Christian movement."
Sean Yost

Jesus was more than serious about the role the Holy Spirit was to play in the disciple's lives. He knew their only hope was the power of His Spirit being in them, on them and flowing through them. Without His power, they would never be able to successfully communicate the gospel message, courageously confront and defeat the demonic kingdom, and furthermore, execute His will on the earth. Jesus put this experience/encounter at the top of the list for His disciples - *"this is your first and highest priority, wait for my power."*

Again, this instruction from Jesus wasn't open for discussion. It was a command, *"Go and wait for my power...."*

So, how does one have an encounter with the Holy Spirit, who clothes, covers, and empowers for victory and service? Jesus described how in Acts 1:5.

*"for John truly **baptized** with water, but you shall be **baptized with the Holy Spirit** not many days from now."*
(emphasis added)

Jesus said He would *"**baptize them (his disciples) with the Holy Spirit.**"*

Baptized? What an interesting choice of words. What was Jesus trying to convey and what did He want us to understand as a result of this word?

All of us have seen people baptized in water. They enter the pool dry but walk out completely drenched. Think about it. Jesus could have used any metaphor to describe what He wanted to do with His disciples, but He chose the word "baptize." Why? Because baptism is a whole body experience; it affects the total person. Again, a water baptism covers every portion of the body, and the person is completely soaked and dripping wet. Get the imagery?

Jesus, in essence, was telling His followers, "I am going to dunk you in My power. You will be completely covered, filled and overflowing with My Spirit." Note: this event is not just a quiet inner experience but also an external encounter that changes a person's total being; nothing is the same, everything is different.

One would have to admit having Jesus "dunk," "immerse," "submerge" and "plunge" you into His Spirit would have life altering ramifications. This baptism isn't an encounter that says, "come to the altar and pray this lovely prayer." No, this "baptism with the Holy Spirit" is aggressive and invasive. Completely revolutionary. No one has ever been left the same after having experienced the baptism of the Holy Spirit.

Have you had this experience?

> *This baptism isn't an encounter that says, "come to the altar and pray this lovely prayer."*

> *"Then the Spirit of the Lord will come upon you, and you will prophesy with them and be turned into another man."*
> 1 Samuel 10:6

POWER TO DIE

Jesus expounds further upon the purpose of the Spirit's baptism.

Acts 1:8,

> *"But you shall receive power when the Holy Spirit has come upon you; and **you shall be witnesses to Me** in Jerusalem, and in all Judea and Samaria, and to the end of the earth."*
> (emphasis added)

Jesus made it clear to the disciples that the baptism with the Holy Spirit would bring exceptional and unusual power to their lives.

He, furthermore, gave an additional reason for this new power: so they could be His "witnesses."

In other words, the disciples would be able to testify and show forth by word and action, what they had seen and heard (Acts 4:20). This power would give them the strength, might, and fearlessness necessary to proclaim the gospel in an unstable religious world filled with hostility toward anything that spoke of and represented the resurrected Christ.

THERE IS MORE

There is more to this word "witness" (Acts 1:8) than one might realize. In the Greek, the word for "witness" is *martus,* from which we get our word *martyr.* It means "one who bears witness by his death."

To us, this may seem to be an unusual interpretation, but don't forget that days earlier the authorities publicly scourged, punished, and brutally murdered their beloved leader. The Roman contingent of soldiers showed no pity, gave no mercy as they viciously ravaged the body of Jesus. This barbaric execution was still fresh in the minds of the disciples when Jesus spoke the words, "you shall be my witnesses...." They clearly understood the impact and the full implication of what Jesus was saying when He used the word *"witnesses"* (martus).

The disciples undoubtedly knew that identifying with, and preaching Jesus' message was a dangerous occupation. The Jews and the Romans were in no mood to deal with another religious movement, much less one that promoted Jesus as the resurrected Messiah. The climate of Jerusalem was charged with an anti-Jesus sentiment. One would think enough is enough. Give it some time so the religious zealots could cool off; perhaps let a few months pass before stirring things up again. That wasn't the plan.

Fifty days after the violent crucifixion, Jesus was equipping His disciples to go right back into the danger zone, to encounter the very ones that crucified Him. He was preparing His followers for the inevitable conflicts and bloody confrontations that were ahead.

> *Fifty days after the violent crucifixion, Jesus was equipping his disciples to go right back into the danger zone...*

He knew for them to survive and thrive they needed His breath permeating every pore of their being. His power would be necessary to face down the threats with daunting, inflexible determination. Jesus knew holy boldness would be needed to stand courageously before the religious leaders and the Roman governing officials. Furthermore, His Spirit would enable them to give an accurate and passionate representation of the love of Christ, to heal diseases and to cast out demons. Nothing short of being supplied with full resurrection power would do.

The disciples agreed and embraced His instruction. The result, they and the world were never the same. Acts 2:1-4 was the event, the outpouring of the Holy Spirit, that changed their lives forever.

MY BAPTISM

I will never forget that September morning when the Lord baptized me with His Holy Spirit. My whole world changed.

I was a Southern Baptist pastor who, at the time was leading one of the fasting growing churches in the State of Georgia. Our ministry was thriving. We were building a new sanctuary, adding new staff and all seemed to be well. However, something began to stir in my heart. Deep down, I knew there had to be more to God than what I was experiencing.

I did something a little risky. I started reading the Bible without wearing my denominational glasses. In other words, I laid aside my Southern Baptist bias as I read the Word. At first, this was difficult for me. All of my life I interpreted the Bible from that perspective...everything was filtered through my Southern Baptist lens. Also, I felt I was betraying my heritage. However, when I committed to doing this, I began seeing new truths, promises, and experiences in the Word that I previously discounted or outright overlooked. The result - I realized I could claim all the promises that were available to the believers in the early church. I could also experience the power they experienced. I discovered God is not a respecter of persons. I could walk in the same spiritual authority they did.

A local pastor heard of my desire to know and experience more of God's power. He got in contact with me and politely invited me to attend a local pastor's Pentecostal prayer meeting. I decided to go. Deep down, I knew this was no place for a Southern Baptist pastor. Only trouble could come from such a meeting. However, my hunger overcame my fears. I went expecting to receive from God.

The men present knew God and His power. After a time of corporate prayer, these men ministered to me and prayed for me. Within minutes the power of God clothed, covered, saturated and filled me. I experienced the baptism with the Holy Spirit (Acts 1:5, 2:4). The very same outpouring of power the disciples experienced, I experienced. It was identical. Everything in my life changed. EVERYTHING!

I would never go back to the way it was before, not for all the money in the world. My experience and baptism with the Holy Spirit was glorious then and remains glorious today!

IT CONTINUES ...

Over the centuries God has been "baptizing people with His Holy Spirit" the same way He baptized Peter, James, and John. Despite what some theologians, scholars and church leaders may say the baptism with the Holy Spirit is still available to those who believe and desire all that God has.

Below are just a few examples of the valiant men God used mightily, all of whom experienced the baptism of the Holy Spirit.

DWIGHT L. MOODY

Dwight L. Moody (1837-1899), was a dynamic highly energetic soul winner. It is estimated that He presented the gospel either by voice or pen to one-hundred million people.[11] His vast preaching schedule took him all over the world and he often preached to crowds of ten thousand to twenty thousand people.

In the midst of Moody's success, an elderly man, whose name we don't know, providentially, confronted the rising evangelist that the

---

[11] Maas, David. "The Life & Times of D.L. Moody." ChristianityToday.com. http://www.christianitytoday.com/history/issues/issue-25/life-times-of-d-l-moody.html.

power of God's Spirit was absent from his ministry. The aging man pointed his finger at Moody and said, "Young man, when you speak again, honor the Holy Ghost."

Not long afterward, while in Chicago, there were two godly women, Mrs. Sara A. Cooke and her friend, Mrs. Hawxhurst, who attended Moody's meetings and insistently prayed for him to be filled with the Spirit.

"Young man, when you speak again, honor the Holy Ghost."

They approached him and said, "We've been praying for you." Moody said, "Why don't you pray for the people?" They answered, "You need power." Moody commented, "I need power? Why I thought I had power." This conversation with these two precious women rattled him to the core. He wasn't able to escape their invasive words, *"You need power."*

Finally, it happened. While on a trip to New York God baptized Moody with the Holy Spirit. Here is what he said of the experience, "Oh, what a day! I cannot describe it; I seldom refer to it; it is almost too sacred an experience to name. I had such an experience of His love that I had to ask Him to stay His hand. I went to preaching again. The sermons were not different, but the servant was! The truths were not new, but now they were pungent and penetrating! A few had been converted before; now converts came by the hundreds."[12]

---

[12] V. Raymond Edman, *They Found the Secret* (Zondervan, 1984) 75.

CHARLES G. FINNEY

Finney was born in 1792 and died in 1875. He became the leader of the 2nd Great Awakening and to this day he is called the "Father of Modern Revivalism." Contemporary pastors and teachers revere his sermons, teachings and thought-provoking quotes.

He too had a life altering and ministry shifting encounter with the Holy Spirit.

After pouring out his heart before the Lord, Finney said, "I received a mighty baptism of the Holy Ghost. The Spirit descended upon me in a manner that seemed to go through me, body and soul. I could feel the impression, like a wave of electricity, going through and through me. Indeed, it seemed to come in waves and waves of liquid love; for I could not express it any other way. It seemed like the very breath of God. I can recollect distinctly that it seemed to fan me, like immense wings." He added, "No words can express the wonderful love that was shed abroad in my heart. These waves came over me, and over me, one after the other, until I recollect I cried out. 'I shall die if these waves continue to pass over me. Lord, I cannot bear anymore.'"[13]

> "I could feel the impression, like a wave of electricity, going through and through me."
>
> Charles G. Finney

---

[13] V. Raymond Edman, *They Found the Secret* (Zondervan, 1984) 43-44.

CHARLES SPURGEON

Many knew him as the "Prince of Preachers." His messages were powerful, inspiring and oftentimes controversial. His ministry influenced the masses and even to this day with great regularity pulpits across the world still reference his life and ministry.

Here is what Spurgeon said about the importance of receiving the Holy Spirit.

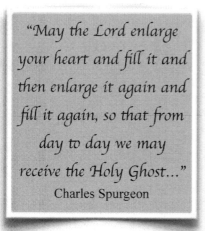

"May the Lord enlarge your heart and fill it and then enlarge it again and fill it again, so that from day to day we may receive the Holy Ghost..."

Charles Spurgeon

"Come let us ask for all that God is willing to give. Does He not say, 'Open thy mouth wide, and I will fill it?' Come, little one, why remain little? Come. You are living on crumbs, why not eat abundantly of the bread of heaven? Do not be content with the pennies when a King's ransom is at our disposal. Poor brother, rise out of your poverty. Sister, bowed down by reason of the little of the Spirit of God you have received, believe for more and pray upon a larger scale. May the Lord enlarge your heart and fill it and then enlarge it again and fill it again, so that from day to day we may receive the Holy Ghost, till at the last, Jesus shall receive us into His glory."

Then he adds, "I would not now be placed back where I was before that blessed experience if you should give me all the world - it would be as the small dust of the balance."[14]

HOW DOES THIS FIT INTO OUR WORLD?

We must note that unless we experience the same baptism of the Holy Spirit that these men and the early disciples experienced our efforts to impact the world will be futile and thoroughly unsuccessful.

> *"I would not now be placed back where I was before that blessed experience if you should give me all the world - it would be as the small dust of the balance."*
> Charles Spurgeon

For over 2,000 years the Church has had the responsibility to display the love and power of Christ in the earth. **Jesus' orders and priority is the same** for us as it was for the original twelve. **He has gifted us the same** way He gifted them, and now, the **SAME POWER** is available to every believer.

Acts 1:8 still applies to our lives and can be experienced, *"I will baptize you with my Holy Spirit so you can have the power to be my witness."*

Here is the result of such a life.

Mark 16:20

> *"And they went out and preached everywhere, the Lord working with them and **confirming the word** through the **accompanying signs**. Amen."*

---

[14] Charles Spurgeon, *What the Holy Spirit Does in a Believer's Life* (Emerald Books, 1993) 114-115.

Acts 6:8

*"And Stephen, full of **faith** and **power**, did great*
wonders and signs among the people. "

The empowerment of the Holy Spirit in our lives must not be deemphasized, explained away, or ignored. The Acts 1:4-8 experience isn't for just a selected few, it is for all believers. Take your denominational glasses off and read the scriptures with no filters. You will be amazed at what you discover.

"Have you received the Holy Spirit
since you've believed?"
Acts 19:2

9.

Next Man Up

"The difference between success and failure is not the will to win.
Everybody has that. The difference is whether
you have the will to prepare to win."
Coach Paul Bear Bryant, Former Head Coach,
University of Alabama

Where I come from, the South, football is a way of life. It seems Saturdays were made for tailgating, backyard football games, barbecue, friends, and college football. There is something incredibly special and entertaining about the sport. Perhaps it is the skill of the young athletes, the intensity of the contest, the rivalries, or just the physical nature of the game. To some, it is a religion.

Recently, on a brisk fall Saturday afternoon, I settled in my home to watch a game between two heated rivals. It was evident from the beginning that this game really mattered to every fan, player and coach. The competition was intense, and the tension and emotion surrounding the game was beyond crazy.

During the first half of the game one team experienced several game-ending injuries to some key players. It truly was alarming to see that many people get hurt in such a short amount of time. It seemed as if every few plays another injured player was being assisted off the field.

I honestly wondered how the team was going to continue to compete at a high level. I felt sorry for the coach and his players. I am sure everyone thought, as I did, that that team was going to lose. Plus, the rest of the year would be a disaster because so many talented players would be unable to play.

At half-time, the coach was leaving the field to address his players in the locker room when a television reporter stopped him for an on-field interview. The reporter, like the rest of us, wanted to know how he and the team would respond to losing so many of his starters to injury. Without hesitating, the coach looked straight at the reporter and said, *"Next man up. Next man up. The next guy has to step up and take their place. We will be all right."* Then he confidently jogged off the field.

I was amazed. In fact, it caught me off guard. I didn't anticipate that kind of a response. Truthfully, I expected the coach to whine and cry about what had happened to his team. Or perhaps, justifiably, make some excuses, even blame others for the injuries. But he didn't. Not a hint of animosity or fear. During the interview, he didn't look nervous or worried that many of his star players were out of the game.

He simply said, *"NEXT MAN UP."*

It made me wonder how he could stay so calm in the face of such devastation. Unquestionably, all the fans were panicking. Why wasn't he panicking? Where were the fear and anxiety? What did this coach know that the rest of us didn't?

HERE IS THE DIFFERENCE

First, he evidently knew his coaching staff had worked hard to prepare all the players for this moment, the game.

Second, each player on the team practiced hard and prepared themselves to play.

Whether or not a team wins a game or has a successful season often depends on a player who hasn't seen much playing time.

If you are familiar with sports, you know the "non-starters," for the most part, watch their teammates play the game. Yes, they are on the team; they wear the same uniform and even cheer for the other players, but usually don't get to play very much. However, things can change quickly, just as it did in the game I was watching.

Whether or not a team wins a game or has a successful season often depends on a player who hasn't seen much playing time. All of a sudden, due to an unforeseen circumstance he is thrust into the game. Everybody, from the coaches to the fans, now look to him because he is the *next man up*. For him, it is his opportunity—his time to step up and do what he has been trained to do.

It is a known fact that coaches constantly stress to their second string players that they are only one play, one injury away from being in the game. Every starting and backup player has to buy into the training and give 100% during practice. Each player knows their mental and physical preparation during the week of practice will determine how they perform on game day.

"When the pressure increases what is engrained in you will come out."
Nick Saban
University of Alabama Head Football Coach

JESUS HAS A PLAN

Following Jesus' resurrection and after countless meetings with Him, the disciples must have thought, "He is back and all is normal again. He is here to stay." But, just as they were settling into their routine and becoming comfortable with Him again at the helm of the movement He did the unthinkable, the unimaginable. He departed.

Right before their very eyes, He ascended into the heavens and vanished out of sight. Within seconds He was gone. No going away party. No parting gifts. Not even time to say "good-bye." Nothing. Everyone was caught off-guard; no one saw this coming. No one expected it. They didn't even get a chance to embrace Him for the last time.

Can you imagine the next few moments after He disappeared from their sight? What were they thinking? Perhaps they were panicked.

Who wouldn't be? Certainly, within the group, they had to have questions:

"What are we going to do?"

"Is He coming back?"

"How can He leave us now?

"Will we survive?"

"Who will lead us?"

"What's next?"

Obviously, this turn of events was difficult for the disciples to understand. It happened so suddenly. However, Jesus knew what He was doing. It was all planned and divinely orchestrated. Yes, for three years He had been the starter, the first string, and the Most Valuable Player. But, He voluntarily removed Himself from the game and now it was time for someone else to step up and continue His work.

> *He voluntarily removed Himself from the game and now it was time for someone else to step up and continue His work.*

In short, Jesus' ascension and departure sent a strong, straightforward message, *"My time is up. I am leaving you. Now it is your turn to preach, teach, love, heal, encourage, and serve. Step up and get the job done."* In other words, **"Next Man Up."**

Let's move the clock forward. Since the resurrection and ascension of Christ and His *sitting down,* Christians throughout the centuries have faithfully committed their lives to serve Jesus and His Kingdom. History books record the incredible stories of men and women of God from every generation who advanced the cause of Christ.

Over the last two millennia, untold millions of devoted believers have courageously shed their blood and laid down their lives for Him. Others left the security of their homes, excellent paying jobs and relocated to the darkest regions of the world to share the gospel with the unreached. Many believers have left booming careers to enter the gospel ministry to preach the Good News. Their service to the Lord came at a tremendous cost with immense personal sacrifice.

While many were called to exotic places to serve Christ, some faithfully served the Master in their community and church. Week after week you could find them passionately teaching the Word of God to their Sunday School class. Others served quietly while greeting people at the entrance of the church, shaking the hands of members and guests alike. Many more would visit the homebound and feed the homeless. There were those who, with no fanfare anxiously visited the jails to share Christ's love with the hopeless. Some would spend hours in intercession for the Pastor and the Church. These precious people represented Jesus and where a conduit of His love and power. They became Jesus' hands, His feet, and His voice.

Right now, these beloved saints of old are in heaven's sweet glory. Collectively, their voices echo through time, and if you listen carefully you can hear them say, **"NEXT MAN UP!"** The seriousness of eternity is ever so real to them. They fully recognize the importance of continuing Christ's work on the earth. They know first-hand the consequences and the risks of inactivity.

SITTING OR STANDING?

We have already learned that the success of a ball team depends on how prepared a player is and how well they do their job when inserted into the game. The same applies when it comes to the body of Christ. But sadly, many in the Church are not prepared and are not ready for service. They have "sat down" rather than "stepped-up." The reasons vary as to why they are not engaged and "in the game." For some it is due to fear, while others feel unqualified, Some are too busy or too tired. Sadly, some just don't see a need. Many others are hoping someone else will step in and do their job for them. These mindsets have to change; too much is at risk.

I heard someone express the severity of the situation this way:

Hell is too hot
Heaven is too real
Eternity is too long
and My responsibility is too great
for me to fail Him in this hour

Friends, we must do more than wear the uniform and enthusiastically cheer from the sidelines. The COACH has called your name. You are the next in line. You must not disappoint those who have gone before and given so much for the cause of Christ. Right now, all of heaven is watching!

Next man up!

10.

"For This I Gave Up Drugs?"

A.W. Tozer said, "If we removed the Holy Spirit from the early church, 95% of what they did would have stopped." He added a stinging indictment regarding the modern church. "If we remove the Holy Spirit from the church today, only 5% of what it does would come to a halt."

Sadly, I believe Tozer's assessment couldn't be truer. Take a close look at the West's version and expression of Christianity. It's polished, professional and for the most part. powerless.

Leonard Ravenhill said, "Christianity today is so subnormal that if any Christian began to act like a normal, New Testament Christian, he would be considered abnormal."

Paul, the quintessential church planter and author of two-thirds of the New Testament, was extremely clear on how the Church should display and represent the message of Jesus to the world. Below is how he said he conducted ministry. I think we can learn a lesson or two.

1 Corinthians 2:4-5

*"And my speech and my preaching were not with **persuasive words** of human wisdom, but in **demonstration of the Spirit and of power**, that your faith should not be in the wisdom of men but in the **power** of God."*
(emphasis added)

1 Corinthians 4:20

*"For the kingdom of God is **not in word** but in **power**."*
(emphasis added)

1 Thessalonians 1:5

*"For our gospel did not come to you **in word only**, but also in **power, and in the Holy Spirit**..."*
(emphasis added)

Wow, these scriptures are powerful. You cannot just scan past these verses; you have to reckon with them, stand toe-to-toe with what Paul was saying about his ministry. They encourage you and yet expose you at the same time. As one studies these passages, you discover three common denominators marked Paul's ministry: the WORD, POWER, and the HOLY SPIRIT.

Paul was making it abundantly clear how he ministered the gospel, "When I come to you, I will not come with fancy, cute, inspiring words only. No, there will be a demonstration (display, show, exposition) of God's Spirit and of power."

Doesn't it stand to reason that if this was Paul's approach to ministry it should be ours as well? Should we not share his expectation and desire?

SO WHAT'S THE PROBLEM?

Where have we missed it?

Don't we preach and worship the same Jesus Paul preached and worshiped? Yes, we do. So why are we not seeing these scriptures manifest in the local church and in our world?

Here are my thoughts. Today the gospel we present to the world is mainly words with little to no physical manifestation of God's might. The question begs to be asked, "Who is to blame for this impotent representation of the gospel?" I believe it belongs on the shoulders of the recent past and current leaders of the church.

Over the last few decades, leaders have created a version of Christianity that is far below that of the experiences found in the New Testament and those of the early Church. Sadly, one cannot deny that the current portrayal of the gospel to the world is well orchestrated, confined, and mostly powerless.

Thomas Aquinas entered the presence of Pope Innocent II before whom a large sum of money was spread out. The Pope observed, "You see, the Church is no longer in that age in which she said, 'Silver and gold have I none.'" "True, holy father," replied Aquinas; "but neither can she any longer say to the lame, 'Rise up and walk.'"

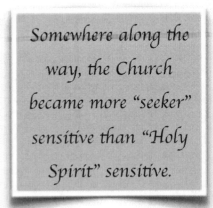

Somewhere along the way, the Church became more "seeker sensitive" than Holy Spirit sensitive. Today, it seems leaders are afraid of offending those who are searching for God. I appreciate their motive. It is admirable because none of us want to be an obstacle to those who are in the process of discovering Jesus. However, too many Pastors in their effort to reach the unsaved have knowingly quarantined the Holy Spirit. They have certain parameters on what is and what isn't acceptable in their services. A significant portion of these leaders are scared that any unscripted manifestation of the Holy Spirit may spook people away from the church. Also, in an effort to control what takes place in the church service, they discourage or forbid the operation of certain gifts of the Spirit. Their reasoning? They don't want anyone to feel uncomfortable. They want to give people a safe place to hear the gospel.

Their actions look to be noble but make zero spiritual sense. Worth noting, neither Paul nor Jesus adopted this style and approach to ministry. In fact, their ministries were anything but "seeker

112

sensitive." Jesus came hiding nothing. He ministered and demonstrated God's power in public and in private. He preached boldly. In many instances, Jesus' message was offensive and problematic to the hearers. He wasn't concerned about triggering negative emotions.

Paul had no "Gospel-lite safe zones." He preached an undiluted gospel and boldly expected God to demonstrate His power in full view of all people. He never confined the movements of God's Spirit in an attempt to win more people.

William Booth who was a Methodist Preacher in the 1800's and founder of the Salvation Army once said, "The chief dangers that will confront the coming century will be religion without The Holy Ghost, Christianity without Christ, forgiveness without repentance, politics without God, and the idea of Heaven without Hell." It seems we are the embodiment of his prophecy.

THE MINISTRY OF JESUS NOT ALLOWED

Truthfully, nearly everything Paul and Jesus did during their ministries would not be allowed to take place in or supported by the majority of the mainline churches in our country. Here is why. Jesus and Paul both exorcised demons, healed the sick, preached more than 30 minutes, laid hands on those needing prayer, raised the dead, addressed sinful behaviors, demanded holiness, and the ultimate no-no, Paul spoke in tongues.

Paul had no "Gospel-lite safe zones"

Isn't it amazing to think that the ministry of the founder, Jesus, and the writer of two-thirds of the New Testament, Paul, would not be allowed or welcomed in our churches? What they preached and how they did ministry would be considered offensive and out of touch with mainline society today?

In my opinion, the "safe church" approach to spreading the gospel has given birth to a neutered church that is grossly anemic. In our attempt to be more attractive to the world we have become fragile, soft and devoid of power.

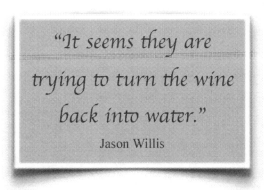

"It seems they are trying to turn the wine back into water."

Jason Willis

Also, to make matters worse, movements and denominations have conveniently created doctrines and theological positions that justify and excuse their lack of power and impotence. Some scholars arrogantly say, "God doesn't do 'that' anymore." Or, "Miracles were necessary then, not now." They add, "Signs and wonders ceased at the death of the last Apostle." My good friend Jason Willis said, "it seems they are trying to turn the wine back into water."

The last time I read the New Testament I didn't recall seeing an expiration date on John 14:12.

"...the works I do, you shall do also."
Jesus

WHEN ARE WE GOING TO DO THE STUFF?

John Wimber was an ex-drug addict who was gloriously saved and eventually became the Founder of the Vineyard Christian Fellowship. Soon after he got saved, he began reading the Bible with great interest and started attending church with his family. For several weeks he observed the seemingly dead worship services. At the conclusion of one of the services, He asked a nearby usher, "When are you going to do the stuff?" The usher looked puzzled and didn't completely understand the question. He replied, "What stuff are you talking about?" Without hesitation, John Wimber said, "The stuff in the New Testament...the miracles, healing the crippled, opening the eyes of the blind and raising the dead. You know, the stuff Jesus did." The usher responded, "Well, we don't do that." Wimber replied, "And for this, I gave up drugs?"

It's not supposed to be this way. Somewhere along the way the gospel underwent a makeover and became severely weakened. Our world is in pain and needs the pure undiluted gospel with zero limitations. Currently, the quiet, quaint presentation of the Gospel is having a detrimental effect on our churches and society. We are losing the battle for the souls of men and will continue to do so if things do not change.

Release the Spirit!

11.

"Playing Church"

---

*"It's about time we quit playing church
in these services that start at eleven o'clock sharp
and end at twelve o'clock dull."*

Vance Havner

I must begin this chapter with a provoking statement by Ed Stetzer, which is indicative of our times, "If people leave impressed with your church but unimpressed with the gospel, you're doing it wrong."

Ouch!

A part of me believes we may be doing it wrong.

Research shows the culture, as a whole, is growing more and more cynical of Christianity. With each passing day, people are becoming more emboldened in their unbelief. Atheism is now a cultural status symbol. People's disregard for the gospel is expanding and they are increasingly more intolerant of our ways and our message. Many in our society see absolutely no reason to embrace our message. Unfortunately, their skepticism may be justified.

The average unbeliever struggles, rightfully so, with the validity and relevance of this 21st-century version of the gospel they are hearing preached. Their mindset and reasoning, "Why should I accept your narrow worldview? Where is the proof your God exists? What difference is your faith making in the world?"

These are legitimate questions and the church must respond.

HOW DID WE GET THIS WAY?

Presently, on many fronts, the gospel of Jesus has been reduced to sermons and messages from well-meaning articulate communicators that tell us what God did in biblical times, what He used to do. However, for the most part, their depiction and understanding of the gospel are frozen in time. In doing so, they inadvertently condition their people not to expect any manifestation of God's power in their life and their church services.

> *Their depiction and understanding of the gospel are frozen in time.*

The Church must never forget that the attractiveness of the Gospel to a lost, hopeless world is the actuality of the power of the Gospel. It's current demonstration. It's present reality. It's nowness. Unbelievers and skeptics are looking for reasons to believe the gospel message. And a demonstration of God's power often is all the evidence they need to become a follower Jesus.

HERE IS THE BIGGEST PROBLEM

Currently, much of the Church is misrepresenting the heartbeat and true nature of the Gospel. We are not seeing an active manifestation of God's presence and power in the lives of believers and their churches. The reason? In part, we have too many narcissistic preachers that are more interested in being culturally relevant than gospel reflective.

> *We have narcissistic preachers that are more interested in being culturally relevant than gospel reflective.*

They measure their worth and effectiveness by how many are attending their church; it has become a numbers game. They are driven by fleshly metrics.

Furthermore, many pastors and church leaders know little to nothing of the fear of the Lord. Fasting, prayer and extended periods of time isolated seeking the face of God is too arduous, time-consuming and seen as an unnecessary, laborious requirement for a gracious God. All the while, endless hours are spent on social media in order to track what's trending and to develop followers. They are obsessed with the tweets and retweets.

THE DIVIDE WIDENS

Sadly, these same messengers step into the pulpit with nothing, no **"thus saith the Lord."** They have speech and nothing more. Have they studied? Yes? Have they prayed? I'm sure they have. But most have not traveled and taken the narrow path to the top of the mountain to meet with God, to hear His voice, to get His message, and to be filled with earth shaking power. But, each week they stand in front of broken, wounded, desperate people. Folks who are in crisis mode, emergency situations. Individuals who are suicidal. Some who have stage-three cancer. Couples whose marriages are coming unraveled. Young people who are cutting themselves. Afflicted addicts are on every row. People who are tormented and bound with fear, guilt, shame and hopelessness come and walk through our hallowed church doors desperately trying to find the God of the Bible. And there, at that moment the man/woman of God stands between the living and the dead.

What is the result? What usually happens?

Unfortunately, too many of these "communicators and professional pastors" have no burning coals in the censer (Numbers 16:46). No power! The fire from the altar has not touched their lips, no sense of eternal urgency in their voice and they are now the disgusting and heartbreaking embodiment of 2 Timothy 3:5, *"having a form of godliness but no power."* They are what Jude 12 describes as *"clouds with no rain."* Or, what Peter says, *"Wells with no water"* (2 Peter 2:17).

> *"A time will come when instead of Shepherds feeding the sheep, the Church will have clowns entertaining the goats."*
> Charles Spurgeon

120

We are now seeing what Charles Spurgeon predicted, "A time will come when instead of Shepherds feeding the sheep, the Church will have clowns entertaining the goats."

TO MAKE MATTERS WORSE

Yes, many of our pastors and leaders have all the right credentials. They graduated from the right schools and have their nicely framed degrees hanging on their office walls. Their bookshelves are overflowing with the who's who in Christendom. They have attended the latest and hottest conferences featuring the most influential pastors in the land. They are forever students seeking to learn more on how to pastor a "successful growing church." Their desire to improve their skill set and understanding is admirable, but it is not enough. We need more than knowledge; we need power! We need God!

Currently, many of these same pastors struggle to call their people to repentance, holiness, and righteousness. To do so would potentially offend seekers and jeopardize their own coolness and threaten the bottom line. They stay in the safe zone of gospel preaching. Feigning hipness and cultural relevance seems to be their idol of choice. They give a steady diet of how to succeed in life. Preaching has become more about their congregant's happiness than their holiness. Too many churches have become like the Dr. Phil or an Oprah Winfrey show. They hear fantastic talks about how to live a good,

> The Gospel has been dumbed down to the point that I am afraid Jesus Himself does not recognize it.

fulfilling life. The listeners are exposed to steps, formulas, and keys that all but guarantee a pleasant experience on earth. However, there is little demonstration of the power God.

For the most part, the Gospel has been dumbed down to the point that I am afraid Jesus Himself does not recognize it.

Today, in our culture, church attendance is more about being blessed, fed, and strengthened. It's about good music, high impact productions, and relevant preaching. In fact, people are invited to come and *enjoy* our services. The mantra: "Come and see how well we do church." Sean Yost describes our current state of existence best, "We have created a Christian market instead of a Christian movement."

Even though church attendance in America is consistently declining, church leaders are doubling down looking for the latest gadgets hoping they will make them more effective, more relevant and more appealing to the lost. Already, we have the latest of everything, apps, laser lights, HD imagery and sound, website, on-line services, holographic imaging, etc. In spite of all these new techniques, every year church attendance is dramatically declining.

Here are some startling statistics.

In 1906, 80% of the American public went to church. By 1986 that number dropped to 40%. Today, less than 18% attend church regularly. It is estimated that less than 10% of the American public will attend church by 2050.

The lost and the searching world does not need our gadgets, our technology, or our state of the art productions. When they come to our church they need to see, feel, and experience the God of the Bible and see His power firsthand.

122

HOW DOES IT CHANGE?

It starts by answering a few probing questions honestly.

Does your soul ache for all of God? All of Him?

Does your private chamber echo the cry of your heart for His resurrection power? If the walls of your prayer room could speak, what would they say of your desperation?

Does your Bible have tear stains from your raw emotion displayed in the presence of God over the lack of power in your ministry? When was the last time you screamed as Isaiah did, "Woe is me!" (Isaiah 6)?

How long has it been since you fasted and denied yourself food until heaven touched you? When is the last time you wept over your church, your city, your own heart?

When was the last time your people have laid prostrate before the Lord openly weeping over the conditions of their bankrupt heart and soul?

Where is your personal altar? Do you have one? Does your church still have one? Or, is it too old-fashioned? Too offensive? Too public? Too messy? Too invasive? Has it been folded and put away? Have we outgrown it? Are we ashamed of it, feel it is unnecessary? Has our desire for dignity deprived us the opportunity to come and die?

Leaders, when was the last time your people have laid prostrate before the Lord openly weeping over the conditions of their bankrupt heart and soul? Again, have we become too sophisticated and culturally sensitive to fall on our faces in public?

Where is the old rugged cross, the dirty towel that beckons us to serve?

Moving Forward: LET'S NOT WATER IT DOWN

We can no longer avoid the heart of God. We must preach the whole gospel of faith, repentance, commitment, sacrifice, obedience, and holiness.

Sadly, it seems these timeless staples of the gospel have been pushed aside for a newer, more relevant, softer gospel. A more palatable version. A less offensive and interfering religion of sorts. Pastors everywhere have eagerly embraced the mindset, "if we *tone it down*, and *take away* the *offensive parts* then people would be attracted to our message." This approach has failed; it hasn't worked nor will it ever.

> "Why do we try so hard to make Jesus cool? He doesn't need a makeover."
> Matt Chandler

Matt Chandler was correct when he answered his own question, "Why do we try so hard to make Jesus cool? He doesn't need a makeover."

IT STARTS TODAY!

It is evident the world doesn't need another trendy preacher or an additional "cool church." No, the world desperately needs a man or woman of God who is filled and overflowing with God's resurrection power, the Holy Spirit. An individual who is committed to walking with God in all of His fullness, no limits, no small print, no excuses.

> *"And when they **had prayed,** the place where they were assembled together was **shaken**; and **they were all filled with the Holy Spirit,** and they **spoke the word of God with boldness.**"*
> Acts 4:31

Make it so LORD. Make it so!

12.

"I Sit in the Upper Deck"

"You were made by God and for God, and until you understand that, life will never make sense."
Rick Warren

Have you ever been exposed to something and then you wished you hadn't? You thought something was going to be great and then you realize, "Oh, no!" For example, when you are at the top of the hill on a roller coaster and you look down and can't see the earth. Or, at a family reunion and it dawns on you that this is your family tree; these are your people. Perhaps it's when you meet your blind date and realize, "This ain't gonna end well."

Right now, I feel that way about a Bible passage. While that might sound weird and a little unnerving, the reality is that Matthew 25:14-30 startles and scares me.

Have you read that story before? No, I mean, have you really read it? Those sixteen verses are riveted with emotion, drama, dread, fear, and many other surprises. There is no gray area here, no allowance for misinterpretation or even room for anyone to water this one down. No one can dodge its undisguised intentions.

WARNING: Buckle up and hang on tight!

KINGDOM OF HEAVEN

Jesus begins His parable in Matthew 25:14, *"For such is the kingdom of heaven."* From the outset, Jesus unapologetically states that the following story communicates how the kingdom of God conducts its affairs, both now and in the future. Don't miss that. He impresses upon His followers: Here is how things will go down for the Kingdom on the earth and afterward.

Jesus' disciples are together, and He proceeds to tell the story of a man preparing to travel to a far country for an extended period of time. The man at the center of this parable is not an ordinary man. He is lavishly wealthy, extremely enterprising and has an established reputation for being a bright and tenacious businessman.

He is lavishly wealthy, extremely enterprising...

Before the wealthy business owner departed for his trip, he gathered three of his most faithful servants and distributed a portion of his resources to each one. The servants obviously had been with their master for some time and had earned his confidence. He knew each one of their strengths and weaknesses. He was well acquainted with their capabilities, as well as their shortcomings. Therefore, each servant received the number of talents based on his ability to manage them (v. 15). He gave one servant five talents, another three, and to the last servant he gave one talent.

The master gave those talents to his servants for a reason. Ultimately, he expected the servants to use the talents to conduct his business affairs in his absence. In other words, to build his business, expand his influence and increase his wealth.

$1.5 MILLION ... OH YEAH!

I'm sure you are wondering how much is a talent? According to the *New Nave's Topical Bible*, one who possessed five talents of gold or silver in biblical times would be a multimillionaire by today's standards. While commentators differ on the exact amount, most agree that during Jesus' time, it would take an ordinary laborer many years to earn just one talent. In our current economy, a talent would be the equivalent of about $300,000.

Let's do the math. The servant with five talents was now responsible for 1.5 million dollars. Boom! That's a lot of money. The guy with two talents was liable for $600,000 and the servant with one talent, $300,000.

A business owner would never give this amount of money to a complete stranger, nor would he give it to someone in whom he does not have complete confidence as to the manner in which to handle it. In the story, it is clear the owner knows the business skill-sets of each servant (v. 15) and has high hopes for them. Also, these servants knew they were expected to use the money given to them to expand the influence of their master and make a profit for him.

THE DRAMA BEGINS

Here is where the story gets interesting. The Master departed after distributing the talents to his servants. We don't know specifically how long the Master was gone. However, in verse 19, Jesus states, *"After a long time the lord of those servants came and **settled** the accounts with them."*

He did what when He returned home?

He ***"settled the accounts with them."*** Uh oh! Not good.

Honestly, this section of the story, and particularly that phrase, makes me feel more than a little uneasy. Every time I read that line my heart races.

What exactly does this mean to *"settle the accounts"*? It is a business term that has profound implications for each of us.

Here are a few definitions for *settle the accounts*: to pay or **receive the balance due;** to pay what is owed; the **collection of payment from what is owed** or **an anticipated return**, to rectify differences and **to measure results according to the prior agreement.**

Every day this type of thing happens in our society. For example, a waiter or waitress who works his or her shift at a restaurant has to "settle up" with the manager or owner at the end of the day.

Here is another example. As a young boy, I had the privilege of selling programs at the University of Alabama football games that were played at Legion Field in Birmingham, Alabama. I entered into a work agreement with the University. It was my responsibility to take a box of programs that were entrusted to me, stand on the street corner and sell the magazines. I made a small profit for each program I sold. Life was good.

Just before the start of the game, after working hard all day, I had to take all the money I had received as a result of selling the programs and meet with the Stadium Administration to rectify my transactions; in other words, to *"settle my account"* with them. If I received 500 programs to sell, I would have to account for each program. If my money was short, the difference would come out of my pocket. In other words, I had to give them what I owed them. I clearly understood they were expecting a profitable return on the programs that were assigned to me. If I did my job well, i.e. if I didn't lose any of the programs and sold them all, they made money, and so did I. As a bonus ... I got into the game for free!

The master left zero doubt that he was expecting some amount of return and growth.

The master/owner mentioned in Matthew 25 wanted to see what "profit" or "earnings" the servants had acquired with his money in his absence. Again, the master left zero doubt that he was expecting some amount of return and growth.

DON'T DIG A HOLE!

In verses 20-25 it is revealed what the three trusted servants accomplished with their portion of the distributed talents. The one who received five talents invested them and doubled the amount. He took 1.5 million dollars and turned it into 3 million dollars. Yes Sir!

The servant who had two talents doubled his money as well. His portion increased from $600,000 to a total of 1.2 million dollars. Nice!

Then the servant who received the one talent went and dug a hole and buried his talent (v. 25). Not good.

The last servant's action is a little puzzling. This servant buried the talent his master gave him. He dug a hole, placed $300,000 in the ground and covered it up.

By all accounts, this seems absurd. At this time in history banks existed, and perhaps credit brokers. At the very least he should have taken the money to the bank for safe keeping. Instead, he took what his master gave him and placed it in the dirt. Certainly, he kept a vigilant eye on that expensive plot of land. Wouldn't you? He had to stand guard to keep it from being stolen. He spent his time protecting rather than producing.

Why did he bury the $300,000? The answer is in verses 24 and 25.

*"Then he who had received the one talent came and said, 'Lord, I knew you to be a hard man, reaping where you have not sown, and gathering where you have not scattered seed. And **I was afraid**, and went and hid your talent in the ground.*

Look, there you have what is yours.'"
(emphasis added)

Paralyzing fear was the underlining impetus for his lack of production.

What caused him to be afraid?

Perhaps it was fear of failure. Or, it could have been that he was afraid of not being able to produce like the other servants. Maybe, in the back of his mind, he was contemplating what would happen to him if he lost all of his master's money in a bad business deal. These are legitimate concerns; however, the bottom line was: He was *scared.* He was *worried* and *frightened* of making a mistake.

HE DIDN'T EVEN TRY

What is most disturbing is that the text gives no indication that he even tried to do anything with the one talent. On all fronts, this was a selfish act on his part. He lived in relative peace, and while he sat and guarded a plot of ground, a piece of dirt, his two other friends labored feverishly to enlarge the influence of their master. He watched. They worked.

Regretfully, he did not fully grasp the honor his master showed by trusting him with such a significant amount of money. He missed the fact that his master recognized distinct qualities in him that signaled his readiness to undertake this task. This servant gave into his fear, and it disabled him. He allowed fear to take away his "ability" to produce for his master.

SHOW AND TELL

Let's look closer. The master *"settled the account"* of each servant. One by one, they stood before their master and made their presentation of what they did with the talents.

They gave an account of their work.

Look at the text. Pay attention to how the first two servants began the conversation, each started the same way, *"Lord, you delivered to me ____ talents; look, I have gained..."* (vv. 20, 22).

> *Their biggest thrill was knowing they had satisfied their master.*

On this, their day of reckoning, they made impressive demonstrations with hard evidence that they grew their master's influence and wealth. Each servant doubled the master's money!

Because of their labor, they heard these words: *"Well done, good and faithful servant; you were faithful over a few things, I will make you ruler over many things"* (Matthew 25:21,23). The master was pleased. Notice he calls them *"good and faithful,"* and then he adds, *"I will make you ruler over many things."* He rewarded them for their performance and hard work.

Imagine how they felt hearing their master recognize their persistent, productive labor. I am sure they were experiencing a broad range of emotions: joy, fulfillment, happiness, and pleasure. Their biggest thrill was knowing they had satisfied their master. They heard what every worker longs to hear from their boss, "WELL DONE!"

After rewarding these two for their impressive achievements, the master turned his attention to the servant who received one talent. After hearing the earnings report from the first two servants, the business owner must have had high hopes for his last employee. The master knew this servant wasn't as "gifted and skilled" as the other servants; this is why he received just one talent. Nonetheless, he still anticipated a positive return on his money. So with eagerness, he waited on the last servant's presentation.

The servant began, and right off the bat it was not good, take a look: *"Lord, I knew you to be a hard man, reaping where you have not sown, and gathering where you have not scattered seed. 25 And I was afraid, and went and hid your talent in the ground. Look, there you have what is yours."* (Matthew 25:24, 25).

Look at those words again, *"I knew you to be a hard man...I was **afraid**...I took your money and **hid it**...I placed what you gave me in the **ground**... (as he rubs and blows the dirt off the money and extends it to the master) here it is all **safe and sound**."*

One must ask, "Really? Is that what you have to offer? That's it? That's how you executed your business plan?" Nothing. Zilch. Goose egg. Zero. Nada. Forty-three words of emptiness.

Not a good response; this isn't going to end well.

> You could actually hear the air being sucked out of the room and see the raging fire in the eyes of the master...

I'm sure you could actually hear the air being sucked out of the room and see the raging fire in the eyes of the master as he heard those words.

What a difference from the first two servants. They said, *"I have gained"* and he said, *"I buried."*

If you read it just the right way, you can almost depict a hint of whining from the servant. (Nobody likes a whiner.)

Talk about underperforming, not doing your job. This guy spoke, but it was all white noise, hot air, excuse after excuse, nothing but hollow rhetoric. What is amazing is that he actually believed he could pull this one over on the boss. Fail.

Truthfully, the saddest part of it all has to be: **he did nothing!**

His fear paralyzed and completely immobilized him.

Here is how his master responded:

> *" 'You **wicked** and **lazy servant**, you knew that I reap*
> *where I have not sown, and gather where I have not scattered seed.*
> ***27** So you ought to have deposited my money with the bankers,*
> *and at my coming I would have received back my own*
> *with interest. **28** Therefore take the talent from him, and*
> *give it to him who has ten talents.*
> ***29** 'For to everyone who has, more will be given, and*
> *he will have abundance; but from him who does not have,*
> *even what he has will be taken away. **30** And cast the*
> ***unprofitable servant** into the outer darkness.*
> *There will be weeping and gnashing of teeth.' "*

BAM! One hundred eight words of pure disappointment, displeasure and disgust.

The master's response was an outright verbal assault on the inaction of the servant. He spoke with no filter, and he did not spare any words. He unapologetically called him **"wicked,"** **"lazy,"** and **"unprofitable."**

Worth noting, there is no hint of grace or mercy; there is no offer of a second chance; there is no consoling or redo and no sensitivity to "feelings." It was a straightforward rebuke that left no chance of misunderstanding disapproval of the master.

He labels the servant as WICKED, LAZY, and UNPROFITABLE.

BREAKING IT DOWN

I completely understand why the master called him lazy, but wicked? Whoa!

We typically connect the word wicked with vile, deviant or lascivious behavior. Worth noting, the master called this servant wicked not for the reason of insidiousness, harmful or disgusting actions, but due to his inaction.

Next, the master calls the servant UNPROFITABLE.

The word *unprofitable* in the Greek is *achreios* which means *"useless, good for nothing."*[15]

---

[15] Blue Letter Bible. "Strong's G888 - *achreios*." https://www.blueletterbible.org/lang/lexicon/lexicon.cfm?Strongs=G888&t=KJV.

The Meriam-Webster Dictionary defines *unprofitable*: "producing no gain, good, or result." It means someone or something is fruitless and ineffective.

Let me break down what the owner was saying to his servant in simple terms. I will paraphrase: *"You are lazy, wicked, unproductive, and unhelpful. Your inactivity has been costly to my cause. I gave you this talent and I have received nothing from you. You are good for nothing and are useless to me."*

The intensity of this tongue-lashing was startling and was unrelenting. The master gave and showed no pity. Then to add insult to injury, the master immediately reminds the servant of his acute business objectives and expectations by rebuking him for not putting the money in the bank so he could at least earn some interest.

27 So you ought to have deposited my money with the bankers, and at my coming I would have received back my own with interest.

He has no one else to blame.

He simply failed to perform.

Our natural reaction is to feel sorry for the servant. Perhaps even to think the master is a little "over the top" or too excessive in his rebuke of the servant. However, the honest conclusion is that the servant brought this spirited reaction upon himself. He has no one else to blame. He simply failed to perform.

NOW WHAT?

Okay, take a deep breath. You will need it. The next question is, "What did the business owner do with the unprofitable servant?"

Read verse 30 carefully.

> *"And **cast** the **unprofitable servant** into the outer darkness. There will be weeping and gnashing of teeth."*

The master's reaction escalates and hits a new level. He loses his patience and becomes more impassioned as he deals with his fruitless servant. He ultimately gave the command to, *"Take from him what he has...and CAST the unprofitable servant into the outer darkness...."*

The Greek word for "cast" (ekballō) implies that one would be thrown out in haste with a notion of violence.[16] He wasn't to be escorted softly, but driven out and expelled. The servant was no longer permitted to be in the group of profitable servants and was ejected from the master's presence.

What a terrible sequence of events. Think about it. Over time, this servant gained the respect of his master. He was invited to be a part of the inner circle. He was hand picked and given the honor and opportunity to increase and manage his master's kingdom. However, as the story reveals, he was overcome by fear and because of his *inactivity* and his failure to perform, his talents were taken away and he was cast into the outer darkness where there is weeping and gnashing of teeth (v. 30).

---

[16] Blue Letter Bible. "Strong's G1544 - *ekballō.*" *https:// www.blueletterbible.org/lang/lexicon/lexicon.cfm?Strongs=G1544&t=KJV.*

HELL OR NOT HELL

People have differing opinions on this text and what the master's words mean when he instructed the servant to be *"cast into outer darkness where there is weeping and gnashing of teeth."* Let me clarify. Some believe that this portion of the passage addresses how God will respond to people who don't know Him, those who are not saved. Therefore, the "unbelieving ones" will be cast into "outer darkness" where there is *weeping and gnashing of teeth."* In other words...hell. One has to make many assumptions, which are not evident in this text if one believes this servant was thrust into hell.

Along with many scholars, I am convinced this servant was not representing an unbeliever being removed from Jesus' presence and cast into an eternal hell. On the contrary, I am certain this servant is a representation of the believer standing before Jesus on the day of judgment (2 Corinthians 5:10). Let's not forget that at the beginning of this chapter, Jesus said, *"For such is the kingdom of heaven."* In other words, this is how the kingdom of God will operate and handle its business. Also, during this entire episode, the master continuously calls the underperforming one his servant. The master maintains his relationship with his servant.

Again, I don't believe the "outer darkness" and "weeping and gnashing of teeth" in this narrative are reflective of this servant being cast into hell, eternally separated from God. Here is what I think is happening. Allow me to use a modern metaphor.

I am a season football ticket holder at the University of Alabama. I receive tickets to every home game in Tuscaloosa. I love being in the stadium with over 100,000 people cheering for Alabama.

My seating assignment in the stadium is predicated on one thing only: my financial contribution to the athletic department of the University of Alabama. Currently, my seat is in the upper deck, I can see the field, but I am not close to the action on the field. The choicest of seats are for those who have given enormous amounts of money to the University.

When I attend a night game, the stadium is flooded with a state-of-the-art lighting system, the best money can buy. Those lights don't shine directly on me. Why? Because I didn't pay enough for the "good seats." The lights light up the field, the players, the coaches and the big dollar boosters. Again, the lights shine over me, not on me. I guess you can say **I sit in outer darkness.** I

> *My seating assignment in the stadium is predicated on one thing only: my financial contribution to the University of Alabama.*

am still in the stadium, but the field and those closest to the field are lit up quite well.

Here is the point: On this day of reckoning and judgment, if Christ determines that someone has been lazy, unproductive, unfruitful, inactive and has wasted the gift He gave them, Jesus will say, "Remove him out of my sight" or "Get him out of here." At that point, the person is removed and escorted to the outer circle, outer darkness, where there will be weeping, gnashing of teeth, and profound remorse for not serving Him wholeheartedly.

This weeping and grinding of the teeth Jesus speaks of in verse 29 is a result of excruciating disappointment and immense sorrow. This regret will be horrific. It will entail sadness that punctures the very core of soul and body. One can only imagine if and when a person hears words of displeasure from their Heavenly Father, every fiber, tissue, muscle and element of their being will be impacted. Anguish, heartache, and mourning like they have never experienced will engulf them.

At that point, the person is removed and escorted to the outer circle where there will be weeping and deep regret for not serving Him wholeheartedly.

Why? Their life is now over. The reality of eternity comes crashing down on them, wave after wave. They see and feel the incredible beauty and love of the Father as He is before them in a full display of honor and unequaled greatness. Just imagine, His countenance is so bright one cannot look. All the while, the truth of the eternal thumps against their chest. They stand in the midst of grandeur, brilliance, and incomparable majesty. Now, they look back at their short, pitiful life lived solely for themselves, full of pride, full of self, full of excuses.

Also, they realize their incessant pursuit of passing pleasure was in vain and full of emptiness. It hits them like a ton of bricks: they have wasted and squandered their one life. Their one chance, one opportunity to show Jesus to the world and serve Him faithfully, boldly and courageously, and they have let it slip away. They have immense regret because now it is revealed that they lived their lives for themselves, for nothing, and not for the KING, the One

142

they now stand before. There are no more days, no more opportunities, no more chances. The full weight of eternity is upon them. With every breath, they woefully cry out in deep agony. They escaped hell. Yes. And they got "in." But they face the realization that they made little to no contribution to the cause of Christ on the earth. The One that saved them now peers deep into their soul.

To make it worse, those who are in this predicament will fully realize *worthy* is the Lamb that was slain. They will hear the hosts of heaven singing and saying, "Worthy! Worthy! Worthy! Worthy is the Lamb of God."

As their eyes scan the heavenly scene, they will be captivated by those present. By the millions, the martyrs are there, their robes white, standing in the midst of their reward (Revelation 6:9,11). The 24 Elders, as well as, the 100 million angels that continuously praise His name are there. All present.

> *Thomas, the one-time doubter, finished strong and faithful. He was thrust through with pine spears, tormented with red-hot plates, and burned alive.*

They will also see the first believers, the disciples, those faithful men who followed Jesus and turned the world upside down for their Master. There is Peter, who was crucified upside down, James, who was executed with a sword, Andrew, who was also crucified. Thomas, the one-time doubter, finished strong and faithful. He was thrust through with pine spears, tormented with red-hot plates, and burned alive. Philip was tortured and then crucified. Matthew was beheaded. Nathaniel was flayed and then crucified. James the Lesser was thrown from the temple and then beaten to death by a club to the head. Simon the Zealot was crucified for his love for Christ. Judas Thaddeus was beaten with sticks until he died. Then there was the Apostle John whom Jesus loved. He was placed into boiling oil. He did not die but was terribly scarred. Next is Stephen, the young deacon in Acts 7 who was stoned to death by religious zealots. Then they see Paul who was beheaded by Nero in Rome.

12 YEAR OLD MARTYR - He is there, too

Recently, twelve Christians in a village outside of Aleppo, Syria were brutally tortured and put to death by the Islamic State, ISIS. Here is the report.

Twelve Christians have been brutally executed by the Islamic State, including the 12-year-old son of a Syrian ministry team leader who had planted nine churches, because they refused to renounce the name of Jesus Christ and embrace Islam. The martyrs were faithful to the very end.

"In front of the team leader and relatives in the crowd, the Islamic extremists cut off the fingertips of the boy and severely beat him, telling his father they would stop the torture only if he, the father, returned to Islam," Christian Aid revealed, according to a report from Morning Star News. "When the team leader refused, relatives said, the ISIS militants also tortured and beat him and the two other ministry workers. The three men and the boy then met their deaths in crucifixion." They were killed for refusing to return to Islam after embracing Christianity, as were the other eight aid workers, including two women, according to Christian Aid. The

eight were taken to a separate site in the village and asked if they would return to Islam. However, after they refused to renounce Christ, the women, ages 29 and 33, were raped before the crowd summoned to watch, and then all eight were beheaded.

They prayed as they knelt before the Islamic State militants, according to the ministry leader Christian Aid assists, who spoke with relatives and villagers while visiting the site. "Villagers said some were praying in the name of Jesus, others said some were praying the Lord's Prayer, and others said some of them lifted their heads to commend their spirits to Jesus," the ministry director told Christian Aid. "One of the women looked up and seemed to be almost smiling as she said, 'Jesus!'" In a manner reflective of Christ's crucifixion, the bodies of those killed were then hung on crosses for display.[17]

These precious believers gave their lives for Jesus. They sacrificed everything for Him. This innocent twelve-year-old boy and his father will be present on the day of reckoning. They will watch as we stand before Him. We will see them, and they will see us. Our commitment and service will unfold for all the world to see. Sadly, for many, this day will reveal a shallow commitment to Jesus. We couldn't get out of bed on a rainy day to attend worship. Or we couldn't tithe due to an overdue power bill. We couldn't serve in the church because of being too tired. Then we see them. Yes, them. The ones who gave it all. In the midst of unimaginable torture and while enduring immense pain, they refused to denounce Him. Those who didn't flinch or hesitate to die for their Savior. We shall stand beside these unbelievable believers. And there we are.

---

[17] Klett, Leah Marieann. " 12 Christians Brutally Executed By ISIS Refused to Renounce Name of Christ, Died Praying, Reciting Lord's Prayer. GospelHerald.com "http://www.gospelherald.com/articles/58293/20151002/12-christians-brutally-executed-by-isis-refused-to-renounce-name-of-christ-died-praying-reciting-lords-prayer.htm.

Our commitment to Jesus will be exposed for all to see. Yes, there will be weeping and gnashing of teeth.

THE CLOCK HAS NO MORE TIME

Those who stand before God in this predicament will realize there is no more time to run the race. It's over. Time has expired. The clock has struck zero. No more opportunities to be faithful, to lay down their life for His cause, to work the harvest, or to serve the King.

At this point the few decades they lived on earth seem so meaningless and trivial as they are on the cusp of eternity, reaping their rewards.

Images of failed opportunities flood their minds. Their thoughts echo, *"Why didn't I do more?"* *"Why didn't I serve Him faithfully?"* *"I should have supported more missionaries."* *"Why didn't I love Him more?"* *"Why didn't I tell others?"* But it is too late. No hitting the reset button; no unplugging and starting over. Tears and regret, you bet. There is no pat on the back. No, "It's all right, you had a tough life." No excuses, no coddling, no participation trophy. It's all business.

Back to the stadium. When I attend the games, I am thankful I am inside the stadium. But if I want a seat closer to the field, the coaches and the game, I must contribute more, give more dollars. Truthfully, where I sit in the stadium is up to me. Better seats, more money. Pretty simple, huh?

13.

"The Day of Reckoning"

"There are two days on my calendar, 'today'
and 'THAT DAY.'"
Martin Luther

Where do we go from here? I think it will be helpful to take an in-depth look at this day of reckoning.

The scriptures make it clear there is coming a day when Jesus, just like the business owner, returns and *"settles the accounts"* with us, His servants. Here are a few passages that forewarn Christians of that day:

Romans 14:10

> *"For we shall **all stand** before the judgment seat of Christ."*
> (emphasis added)

Romans 14:12

*"So then **each of us shall give account of himself** to God."*
(emphasis added)

1 Corinthians 3:12-15

*12. Now if anyone builds on this foundation with gold, silver, precious stones, wood, hay, straw, 13. each one's work will become clear; for **the Day** will **declare it**, because it will be **revealed by fire;** and the fire will test **each one's work,** of what sort it is. 14. If anyone's work which he has built on it endures, he will receive a **reward.** 15. If anyone's work is burned, he will **suffer loss;** but he himself will be saved, **yet so as through fire."***
(emphasis added)

2 Corinthians 5:10

*"For we must **all appear** before the judgment seat of Christ, that **each one may receive** the things done in the body, **according to what he has done**, whether good or bad."*
(emphasis added)

The phrase "judgment seat of Christ" appears in the above texts as the Greek word *"bema."* In the Greek culture, *bema* referred to an elevated platform from which victorious athletes received their crowns. In the New Testament the *bema seat* is a place of pronouncing award or punishment as demonstrated with Pilate (Matthew 27:19; John 19:13), Herod (Acts 12:21), Festus (Acts 25:6, 10, 17), and Gallio (Acts 18:12, 16, 17). As you can see, the *bema seat* had many purposes; in some cases, it was used to award an individual and in other situations to exonerate and even to condemn.

First, Paul writes to his fellow believers in Corinth (1 Corinthians 3:13f) to remind them of an upcoming event he called "the Day." He warns them that on that day our works will be declared and shown openly. They will be revealed, uncovered, and each work will be tested by fire. Each person's labor for Christ will be meticulously analyzed and scrutinized by the Father. And the believer will either receive a reward for their work or suffer loss (1 Corinthians 3:14-15).

To suffer loss means that the one being judged will experience detriment; their eternal rewards suffer, sustain damage, and are injured. And in many cases forfeited altogether. Let us recall what happened to the unproductive servant in Matthew 25.

> **28** *"Therefore take the talent from him, and give it to him who has ten talents.* **29** *For to everyone who has, more will be given, and he will have abundance; but from him who does not have, even what he has will be taken away."*

The unproductive servant suffered loss on multiple fronts. Once again, this Day of Judgment is severe and all Christians should analyze their walk with the Lord and prepare themselves accordingly.

Secondly, in 2 Corinthians 5:10, Paul gives additional insight to the Church at Corinth with regard to this Day of Judgment. This text states we must "all appear" before the great judgment bar of God. The word **"appear"** is significant. The Greek word is *phaneroo,* and it means, *to make manifest, to make clear, to make visible, or to reveal.* Philip E. Hughes, commenting on the meaning of *phaneroo* writes, "To be made manifest means not just to appear, but to be laid bare, stripped of every outward façade of respectability, and openly revealed in the full and true reality of one's character."[18] God will look deep into our lives and inspect our hearts and analyze how we served Him.

As we shall continue to see, the day of settling the accounts isn't all butterflies and roses. It is a time of great revelation and exposure.

Paul says that the individual who is appearing before God will "receive the things done in his body...." What is interesting is that the word *receive* comes from a form of the verb *komizo,* which means, *to receive back what is due.* Knowing the true meaning of these words makes it easier for us to understand what the Master in Matthew 25 did with his servant when he settled the account with him.

If one is not careful, after reading 2 Corinthians 5:10, a person may become confused and misunderstand the purpose of this judgment. I will attempt to bring understanding. First, this judgment ISN'T about a Christian's sin. Second, this judgment is solely about performance and what the believer did for the Master.

Some well-meaning people believe because the word "bad" is in the text that it must mean *sin.* However, the word *bad* in 2 Corinthians 5:10 is κακός which is not the word commonly used for sin and/or missing the mark, that word is *hamartia.* κακός can be interpreted to imply *worthless,* which is the none effect of ones behavior, or "injurious." Furthermore, often the word translated for *bad* in the Interlinear Greek New Testament is *phaulos,* which is a synonym for κακός and phaulos, which means *worthless, of no*

[18] *The Second Epistle to the Corinthians,* The New International Commentary on the New Testament [Grand Rapids: Eerdmans, 1992], 180.

value injurious, and/or useless. Richard C. Trench writes that *phaulos* "contemplates evil under another aspect, not so much that either of active or passive malignity, but that rather of its good-for-nothingness, the impossibility of any true gain coming forth from it."[19] It is in this context we must understand the word "bad."

The business owner in Matthew 25 became indignant toward his servant not because of malicious intent to harm his kingdom, but rather due to his indifference and inactivity. It led the master to say, *"You are wicked, lazy, and unprofitable."*

Correctly defining the words used in the above texts help clarify that the future judgment will not deal with our sin but rather our activity and usefulness in the work of God. The point is clear. There will be complete exposure of the things we *are* or *are not* doing for His kingdom. Those things we are putting in front of our service for the King, worthless activities, and things that have no eternal value will all come to light on that day.

John the disciple said in 1 John 2:28,

> *"And now, little children, abide in Him, that when He appears, we may have confidence and **not be ashamed** before Him at His coming."*

In the treasured book of 1 John, the Apostle was warning us of a day when Jesus will come and *settle the accounts* with His children. In this text, the beloved disciple sounds the alarm and flashes the lights encouraging us to prepare for that day so that when we stand before Him we will not be ashamed.

---

[19] *Synonyms of the New Testament* [Reprint; Grand Rapids: Eerdmans, 1983], 317.

According to Thayer's Greek Lexicon, *ashamed* means to *dishonor* or *disgrace*. It implies that those who do not remain faithful to the end and work for Christ will be dishonored or disgraced, just like the unprofitable servant in Matthew 25.

Throughout the New Testament, God has used multiple texts from various authors to prepare Christians for the judgment to come. The language He uses is straightforward and leaves no room for speculation.

Revelation 22:12 further emphasizes the realization that Jesus is going to judge and give to us according to how we served Him, nothing more. The Word is emphatic about how God will react to how we lived our lives. He states,

> *"And behold, I am coming quickly, and My **reward** is with Me, to give to every one **according to his work**."*
> (emphasis added)

Some Christians believe, "It doesn't matter what I do on the earth, as long as I am saved all is good." Too many believers embrace that lie. The above-referenced texts have made an indisputable case for our appearing before God to give a report of what we did for Christ on the earth.

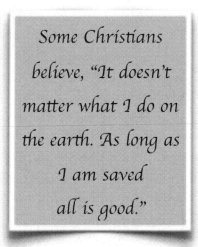

Some Christians believe, "It doesn't matter what I do on the earth. As long as I am saved all is good."

No one can deny that Jesus expects fruit and diligent service from His followers (John 15:8). He wants us to faithfully represent Him. He longs for us to use our lives for His glory, to expand His influence, to labor faithfully for Him in His Church.

IT'S CLOSER NOW THAN EVER

How well are you doing? What have you done with the gift He gave you?

The day is fast approaching when He will summon us to His great seat. He will *settle our account.* He will expect a return on His investment. Never forget our contribution to His work will determine how He responds to us on that day, along with our future responsibilities in heaven.

Let's serve Him well so we can hear on that day, "WELL DONE, good and faithful servant!"

14.

"It's Not the Devil's Fault"

"Church, we are plan A and there is no plan B."
David Platt

"When you're hot, you're hot; when you're not, you're not." Geraldine Jones made this phrase popular during the 1970's.

As a kid growing up, I used to beg my parents to postpone bedtime so I could watch a popular TV variety show called "The Flip Wilson Show." Flip Wilson, who played Geraldine Jones, developed several sayings that became national catchphrases. Another popular phrase was "What you see is what you get." I can still see and hear him saying these lines. These were iconic statements. However, his best catch phrase and the one that made him nationally famous was, "The devil made me do it." It never failed. During each show, he would say that phrase. It was like clockwork. Everyone anticipated the moment, and every single time he said it the audience would breakout wild with laughter.

This culture-shaping slogan was so popular in the 60's that thousands of people wore t-shirts with that phrase on the front. Talk about a fashion statement! Sadly, this six-word phrase changed how people defended their behavior. It molded their approach to life. Folks starting looking at their conditions in life differently. Think about it…what a great excuse! It's no longer my fault. I had no choice. *"The devil made me do it."* The crowd and America loved it.

WE LIKE IT TOO

Just like on the show, it seems the church world is quick to blame the devil for our problems and especially the world's current state of affairs. No doubt, the devil certainly deserves some of the blame. We all know first hand he has distributed more than his share of pain and despair. However, I think he gets way too much credit; some of the stuff happening just isn't his fault. Let me explain.

It doesn't take a rocket scientist to come to the conclusion that the complexity of issues the world is facing isn't solely the responsibility of the devil, or a disinterested and disengaged

…the responsibility for the condition of the world falls directly in the lap of the Church, Christ's body.

156

deity. I think you would agree that humanity, us, over the years, without any assistance from outside "spiritual" sources have messed things up pretty well. Also, I firmly believe a significant portion of the responsibility for the condition of our world falls directly in the lap of the Church, Christ's body.

Here are the reasons why I believe the church must assume a large amount of the responsibility for the grim condition of our world. First, many leaders and denominations have failed to preach the whole counsel of God. We have preached and taught portions of the Word, but not all. Second, we have not challenged our people to experience more, and to do and believe for more. In my opinion, this has severely limited the opportunities God has had to express Himself to the world, which He desperately

> *When the truth is filtered, and the light is limited darkness and evil flourishes.*

desires to do. You ask, "Is that even possible to limit God and His activity?" Here is what the Psalmist Asaph said,

> *"Yes, again and again they tempted God,*
> *And limited the Holy One of Israel."*
> (Psalm 78:41)

One cannot deny that our lack of being taught what God can and desires to do with and through His people has led to a substantial void in the demonstrations of the power of God. Thus, God's movement has been hampered throughout the world. The body of Christ has learned the hard way that when the truth gets filtered and the light is limited, darkness and evil flourishes.

To make matters worse, it appears some of the professional religious intelligentsia, denominations/movements and some members of the church, for whatever their justification may have been decided that the church needed to "tone" things down. Their goal was to create a more palatable gospel, one that would be more inclusive and less intrusive. A gospel that was softer, a version, if you will, that wasn't as counter-culture as the one the early disciples represented. One with fewer rough edges that

> *The attempt to make the gospel relevant has inadvertently caused the gospel to lose it's relevance.*

didn't require as much from the adherent. They wanted this new version of the gospel to be more sophisticated and culturally relevant. Pastors and speakers changed what they said and how they said it because they wanted to make the gospel more attractive in order to to enlarge its reach and receptivity. These efforts to modernize the gospel has not helped us reach more people. In fact, now, fewer and fewer people are interested in our watered-down version of the gospel. We have so filtered the light of the gospel that it no longer attracts desperate sinners. The attempt to make the gospel relevant has inadvertently caused the gospel to lose its relevance.

Over time the devil's ultimate aim has been to render the Church powerless, stationary, useless, and ineffective. Honestly, it looks like the devil didn't even have to lift his finger to get us to this point. We have done the his work for him. Over the last few decades, the gospel has been institutionally and systematically weakened.

158

History is a harsh reminder that when the Church of the Living God does not express the full gospel, people fill the void with false gods, anomalies and mutated renditions of the pure gospel. This horrific absence leads to empty religious exercises that are meaningless, powerless and emotionless. Churches become cold and sterile, and eventually, societies slowly migrate into unimaginable behavior, brutal violence, abhorrent hatred, reprehensible perversion, and darkness. Right now our culture is experiencing everything mentioned above.

> ...it looks like the devil didn't even have to lift his finger to get us to this point, we have done his work for him.

We cannot afford to be on the wrong side of history. My prayer is that this generation will create a new standard and faithfully display the great acts of God on the earth-the type of exploits that would even impress the first-century disciples.

Oh, that God would answer the prayer of the beloved John Wesley, "Give me 100 preachers who fear nothing but sin and desire nothing but God; such alone will shake the gates of hell."

2 Chronicles 16:9

> *"For the eyes of the Lord run to and fro throughout the whole earth, to show Himself strong on behalf of those whose heart is loyal to Him."*
> (emphasis added)

Deuteronomy 11:32

*"...the people who know their God shall be strong,
and **carry out** great exploits..."*
(emphasis added)

Make it so, Lord!

15.

"God Has

BIG Plans"

Here is a startling revelation that will raise some eyebrows:

**"While we (the Church) are waiting on God
to get things done, God is waiting on the church
to get things done."**

Contrary to what some Christians believe, Christianity is more than attending a church service once a week and experiencing a warm fuzzy feeling. To many, this seems to be the prevailing perception of why the Church exists.

In reality, God looks to us to represent Him and to faithfully execute His will on the earth. Sadly, due to our misunderstanding or innocent ignorance of His method of operation, His plan and desire for the world is not being fulfilled. His will is largely going undone and it isn't His fault.

Augustine, who's ideas and concepts greatly influenced Western Christianity, was correct when he stated,

> "Without God, we CANNOT,
> without us, GOD WILL NOT."

The body of Christ must understand that when we do God's work that God works with us and through us. He doesn't work *instead of* us and *independent of* us but chooses to work in *cooperation* with us. For example, Mark 16:20 says,

> *"And they went out and preached everywhere,*
> **the Lord working with them** *and confirming the word*
> *through the accompanying signs."*

Here is the context. Mark wrote that, after Jesus ascended into heaven and sat down, *"they went out and preached the Word."*

Who went? The disciples.

They courageously traveled to the villages and the surrounding cities to share the news of the resurrection of Christ. Here is the key point: As they went, the Lord *"worked with them."*

The three English words, "worked with them" is the one Greek word *synergeō*. The Greek meaning is "to work together, to partner in labor, to put forth power together, to assist."[20]

It is imperative that we fully understand the significance of what God did with the disciples as they went: He *assisted, joined* and *partnered* with them as they preached and ministered. He combined His spiritual power with their physical power. He worked in cooperation with them so others could hear and be healed.

What is further interesting, the Greek word *synergeō* is where we get our English word *synergy* which means, "the interaction of two or more agents or forces so that their **combined** effect is **greater than** the sum of their **individual** effects."[21] Synergy is another way of saying, "teamwork, alliance, combined effort and strategic union."

God could have chosen any word to describe what happened but He strategically used this particular word in this context to open our understanding as to how God works in collaboration with His Church to impact the world. He doesn't operate alone, but in willing alliance with His children. This is simply amazing.

> *He combined His spiritual power with their physical power.*

---

20 Blue Letter Bible. "Strong's G4903 - *synergeō.*" https://www.blueletterbible.org/lang/Lexicon/Lexicon.cfm?strongs=G4903&t=KJV.

21 Oxford Dictionaries, *s.v.* "synergy," http://www.oxforddictionaries.com/us/definition/american_english/synergy.

It gets even better.

Mark adds that, as the disciples ministered for Jesus, *"God confirmed the word [their preaching] with accompanying signs."* Because they were working in perfect union *with* God, God gladly worked *with them* and certified their preaching by displaying His power through miracles, supernatural expressions, and life change.

SUPER GOOD NEWS!

If this is the way Jesus used His followers at the start, I have to believe this is the way He desires to use his followers now. However, some well-meaning theologians, scholars, teachers, and pastors would vehemently disagree with my hopeful outlook. They have a difficult time believing God would choose to use people today the same way He used the early disciples. They firmly hold to the idea that God doesn't need man at all. Furthermore, some believe that miracles have passed and certain gifts of the Spirit are no longer valid and necessary.

In my humble opinion, to embrace and believe such a viewpoint is ludicrous, reckless, and dangerous.

I choose to look at the Bible with anticipation and a healthy expectation. Plus, I say, why couldn't He do more now than He did at the beginning? Or better yet, why wouldn't He? Are we not in the last days? Don't you typically save your best for last? Isn't it true that people are not known for how well they started but how strong they finished?

NO TIME TO CUT BACK

Consider the following:

- Today, right now, there are nearly 3 billion people on the earth who have not heard a clear presentation of the gospel.[22] All the while, it is estimated that an American, on average, will hear the gospel thirteen times before they die.

- When Jesus lived there were approximately 300 million people on the planet.

- There are more people alive right now that have never even heard the name of Jesus than were alive at the time Jesus lived. *You may want to reread that sentence.*

Did you know that right now there are more people on the earth who have never even heard the "name of Jesus" than were alive at the time Jesus lived?

- 337 of the 550 people groups in China do not have even Bible portions available in their primary language.[23]

---

22 Baxter, Dr. Jeff. "2.87 Billion People Have Never Heard the Gospel." SacredOutfitter.blogspot.com. http://sacredoutfitter.blogspot.com/2013/03/287-billion-people-have-never-heard.html.

23 Joshua Project. "Global Statistics." JoshuaProject.net. https://joshuaproject.net/global_statistics.

- There are some 458,000 villages in India with no known Christian presence.[24]

- In the last 40 years over 1 billion people have died who have never heard of Jesus and close to 25 million will perish this year without hearing the wonderful story of salvation.[25]

These statistics strongly prove that the world is grossly unreached.

So, in my opinion, this is not the time for God to cut back on His expressions of power to the unsaved world. This is not the moment for God to do less. Nor is it time for us to limit what God can do through believers. It is the perfect season to believe God for more and expect for more.

In this late hour God is beckoning men and women to share His love with the billions of lost souls on the earth. His heart aches for them and He will do anything to reach them. He just needs an obedient individual to use. And those who surrender their lives for His purpose will be endued with supernatural power unlike the world has ever seen.

IT BEGINS HERE

The secret to the Lord's success lies with the awareness that God uses His children to spread His message.

We are His body (1 Corinthians 12:27).

---

[24] Joshua Project. "Global Statistics." JoshuaProject.net. https://joshuaproject.net/global_statistics.

[25] "The Coming Revolution, R. Mark Baxter, p. 12.

We are His witnesses (Acts 1:8).

We are His ambassadors (2 Corinthians 5:20).

Our assignment is clear. But what happens if the church doesn't respond and we don't do our part?

Answer:

If we do nothing, nothing gets done.

If we sit, He sits.

If we say nothing, nothing is said.

If we delay, He is delayed. Period.

If we don't pray, Heaven doesn't respond.

If we don't move, He doesn't move.

If we don't serve, He doesn't get to serve.

If we don't witness, His word doesn't get shared.

Truth be told, you and I are the ones who limit God's effectiveness on the earth, not sinners, not the devil. Us.

God has big plans for the church in these last days. We must return to the power of the early disciples. God is more than ready to pour out His Spirit on us.

I believe Acts 2:17,

> *"And it shall come to pass **in the last days**, says God,*
> *That I will pour out of My Spirit on all flesh..."*

The best is yet to come!

16.

They Could Not

---

*"Two things: We can never do what only God can do
and God will never do what He has asked us to do."*
Todd Smith

Jesus selected Peter, James, and John to join Him for prayer at the
top of the mountain. We affectionately know this event as the
Mount of Transfiguration (Matthew 17). However, while Jesus was
meeting with them, plus Elijah and Moses, a stunning event was
unfolding at the base of the mountain.

A father in desperate need had a young son who was being
viciously tormented by a demon. On occasion, the demon would
cause epileptic type seizures. These seizures would cause the
young boy to fall into fires, burning him severely. The father
reported that the demon would also cause his son to fall into water
in an effort to kill him (v.15). These disturbing events had to be
horrible for his father and family to witness. The dad continuously

169

feared for his precious son's life. He loved his son, and as any good parent would, he desperately longed to see his boy healed and set free from this unmerciful demon.

Having heard of Jesus to be a successful exorcist, the father had come hoping for a cure for his boy. When Jesus could not be found the father did the next best thing. He took his son to Jesus' adherents, His disciples, so they could heal the child.

On all fronts, this was an appropriate course of action since the disciples had been with Jesus, worked closely with Him and had been entrusted with authority and power to cast out demons. Matthew 10:1 states, "that *when He had called His twelve disciples to Him, He gave them power over unclean spirits, to cast them out, and to heal all kinds of sickness and all kinds of disease.*"

> *No one told the demon to cooperate with their plans.*

NOT SO FAST

After hearing of the boy's condition, Jesus' followers assumed this case of "demonic possession" would be no different than the others…say a few words, pray, give the command of faith and then boom, the boy would receive his freedom, and things would get back to normal. However, there was a slight problem. No one told the demon to cooperate with their plans. As if on point, the disciples did the routine, they followed the script. Everything that worked before, they attempted.

But nothing happened this time. No change. I'm sure they prayed to God and shouted at the demon multiple times commanding it to leave, but the demon didn't budge. They were unsuccessful. Nothing they attempted seemed to work. Unfortunately, the precious boy remained the same, still tormented.

Needless to say, the father and the disciples were highly disappointed with the lack of results. Without a doubt, the father had to be brokenhearted and discouraged, but he did not give up hope. He bravely and patiently waited for Jesus to descend from the mountain.

Meanwhile, as the father's disappointment became apparent, a concerned, passionate crowd had gathered. People wanted to know what was going on. The disciples found themselves surrounded by an angry mob, and before they knew it, they became entangled in a full-blown religious argument with the scribes and all that were present. No doubt, the scribes took advantage of the opportunity to call into question the disciple's faith, their theology, their allegiance to Judaism and above all, their controversial leader. This only added fuel to the fire. The dialogue between the religious leaders and the disciples heated up rather quickly and went from bad to worse. Not good. The scene was escalating out of control (Mark 9:14).

HE APPEARED...

After Jesus' glorious mountaintop experience, He and the three others came to the bottom of the mountain to find chaos abounding. While the scribes and disciples were arguing, Jesus accessed the situation and wanted to know what was going on. Before the scribes and disciples could present their cases, the father of the demonized boy, obviously overwhelmed with hope, humbly approached Jesus, knelt down and said,

"Lord, have mercy on my son, for he is an epileptic
and suffers severely; for he often falls into the fire and often into
the water. 16 So I brought him to Your disciples,
but they could not cure him."
(Matthew 17:15, 16)

"They
    could
        not
            cure
                him."

Ouch!

What a punch in the gut, *"They could not...."*

I'm sure the father wasn't trying to get the disciples into trouble. He was just stating the fact that the disciples could not help him. He simply wanted his son to be made well.

This honest criticism was a severe blow to both Jesus and the disciples. How? It uncovered the disciples' inabilities and shortcomings.

Let it be noted; nobody doubts the disciples' desire to help this troubled family. Apparently, they tried. They get an "A" for effort. But, they were ineffective. The boy was unchanged. The destructive demon remained.

No one was more frustrated with the results of this encounter than Jesus. You can imagine His disappointment when He heard the

> *This event highlighted weaknesses that He wanted to be corrected.*

words, *"I took him to your disciples, but they could not cure him."*

How would Jesus respond to such a scathing report against His beloved followers? Would Jesus be defensive or perhaps ignore the comment altogether? Jesus did neither.

Jesus addressed the issue publicly (v. 17) and privately (vv. 19-21).

Publicly He got straight to the point. Immediately after hearing the father's report Jesus said,

> *" 'O **faithless** and **perverse generation** how long shall I be with you? How long shall I bear with you?*
> *Bring him here to Me.' "*
> Matthew 17:17

His rebuke to His disciples was sharp, and it cut deep.

First, He calls them *faithless*. The Greek word He used is *apistos*, meaning faithless, unbelieving.

I know what you are thinking. How is this even possible? How can you walk with Jesus and see first hand all the miracles He performed and not have faith? Evidently, it's possible.

Second, He calls them a *perverse generation.*

Whoa! That's intense. Did Jesus just say that about His closest friends? I get the "unbelieving" part. No problem. But to call them "perverse" seems a little harsh and excessive.

173

So what was Jesus implying?

To fully understand why Jesus used the word perverse, the context of Jesus' rebuke needs to be taken into consideration. His scolding isn't to the outsiders, the arguing scribes, or the casual observers who witnessed this event. His disapproval is for His followers. If we are not careful, we will miss Jesus' intent and the reason He used this particular word to describe the behavior of His disciples.

Initially, when we see this word we think perversion is to only mean repulsive behavior, wickedness, debauchery, total disregard for purity and deep dark sin. However, in this text, the Greek word for *perverse* is *diastrepho*. It means to distort, turn aside, and to misinterpret.

The dictionary defines perverse as *to go counter to what is expected or desired.*

I'm convinced Jesus didn't rebuke them because of their indecent fleshly indulgences, but rather, due to their lack of understanding and cooperation with His will.

Again, the word perverse doesn't always mean wicked or deviant behavior. When you take a closer look at the synonyms for "perverse" you can fully understand what Jesus was trying to communicate to His disciples:

CONTRARY,
UNCOOPERATIVE,
UNHELPFUL, and
OBSTRUCTIVE.

Here is my expanded attempt to describe the intensity and purpose of what Jesus was saying to His disciples:

"Your lack of cooperating with me has distorted my purpose. You have stood in the way of my plan for this boy. I couldn't heal him because of you. You were not helpful. You detoured my purpose and power and corrupted my intent. Your failure to execute my will acted as a deterrent."

It is important to notice that Jesus didn't place blame for the lack of healing on the father or even the young boy, Jesus points the finger directly at His partners.

He questions their faith.

> *"Then Jesus answered and said,*
> *'O faithless and perverse generation **how long shall I**
> **be with you? How long shall I bear with you?***
> *Bring him here to Me.'"*
> Matthew 17:17

Make no mistake about it; Jesus was not happy with how His disciples handled this opportunity. He was hoping they were more advanced in understanding their authority and role in propagating His heart and purpose. He firmly believed they should have been able to meet this need and set the boy free.

> *"You have stood in the way of my plan for this boy."*
> Jesus

Jesus probed deeper as His rebuke continued. He vented some of his frustration by asking two rhetorical questions,

"...how long shall I be with you? How long shall I bear with you?"

What is Jesus' purpose for these two questions?

The in-depth answer is found in the word, *bear*. In the Greek it means, *to hold up, to sustain.*

Jesus was saying, *"How long am I going to have to hold you up, bolster, prop you up, and continue to do this work for you?"*

In addition, Jesus was saying, *"You are going to have to grow up so you can stand up on your own and do this."*

Again, it is evident Jesus was not pleased with their ineffectiveness. He had hoped for more, much more.

With this rebuke Jesus was wanting His group to realize and hear the following:

"I need you to understand I want to use you to minister to hurting people. Stop relying on me to do everything. You constantly depend on me to do these type of things. I have trained you; I have given you authority...My authority. You have watched me and have learned my ways. I am going to depart soon; I am not going to be here in my flesh and bone body, I will not be able to rescue you. How are you going to confront and defeat the powers of evil when I'm gone?"

Ultimately, He had envisioned they would have accurately represented Him and brought the healing power of the Kingdom of God to this hurting father and his demonized son, *"but they could not."*

WHAT WENT WRONG?

Later that evening the disciples, confused as to their lack of results, asked Jesus the question in v. 19, "why *could* we *not* cast the demon out?"

Here is Jesus' response (vv. 20-21),

> *"Because of your **unbelief**...I say to you, **if you have faith**
> as a mustard seed, you will say to this mountain,
> 'Move from here to there,' and it will move;
> and **nothing will be impossible for you**. 21. However, this
> kind does not go out except by **prayer and fasting**."*

A fact worth noting: Even though the disciples had God-given authority to cast out demons (Matthew 10), their authority was ineffective because they lacked the necessary faith.

God is attracted to faith! Remember, without faith, it is impossible to please Him (Hebrews 11:6). And with faith, nothing will be impossible! (Matthew 17:20).

WE HAVE TO TAKE THIS SERIOUSLY

As the world grows more hostile toward God and enters into unprecedented wickedness the church must be filled with faith. A weak, anemic faith will be no match to the wiles and schemes of the enemy. A bold, strong and courageous faith will be necessary.

The world needs the church to have usable faith. A faith that gets results. Honestly, I wonder how many tormented souls have entered our church doors needing a touch from God but left the same way they came because WE COULD NOT CURE THEM? Perhaps they heard an encouraging word but encountered no power.

These results have to change, and they have to change now. We have to do better.

How does this type of faith come?

The list below is not exhaustive, but the Scriptures reveal that these three things are necessary to build your faith.

1. A Consistent Intake of the Word of God.

Romans 10:17 states, *"Faith comes by hearing and hearing the word of God."* Without the Word you will not know His promises, nor will you know the full reach and potential of your authority. The devil fears the Word and will work diligently to keep you from it. When you know the Word and use it in faith, Heaven responds.

> *...how many tormented souls have entered our church doors needing a touch from God but left the same way they came...?*

Note: if you have not deposited the Word of God into your Spirit, you will be unable withdraw it when you need it.

2. A Continuous Spirit of Prayer.

In Mark's account of this event, verse 29, Jesus said, *"This kind [of demon] can come out only by prayer and fasting."* These words seem to indicate that the disciples did not spend enough time in prayer. One is left to believe they didn't take prayer seriously. Surprising! Why didn't they pray before engaging in such a severe spiritual battle? Did they assume their past victories would automatically assure future victories?

Meeting with God is a necessary component to walk in His power. Daily communion with God develops faith, plus a hearing ear. Why is this necessary? At times God will whisper His instruction and wishes to you. You must be acquainted with His voice. Jesus said, *"My sheep hear my voice"* (John 10:27).

Jesus taught His disciples this valuable lesson in Matthew 10:27:

"Whatever I tell you in the dark, speak in the light; and what you hear in the ear, preach on the housetops."

If we are unfamiliar with His voice, we will miss "God opportunities" for healing and restoration. The more time spent in prayer will enable us to develop a keen sensitivity to His promptings. We will experience a new level of usefulness.

3. A Commitment to Fasting.

Just like the disciples, you and I will face some formidable demonic spirits. Many of these confrontations will demand a deeper authority and greater faith from us. For us to attain the level of faith and authority necessary to confront and defeat the enemy, we will need to fast.

179

Let's face it. Fasting is painful. It is not on top of our list of favorite things to do. However, I have realized that fasting is not my enemy, but my friend.

Fasting enables us to deny our fleshly desires so we can position ourselves for greater usefulness. Living a "fasted lifestyle" keeps you in-tune and prepared for ministry.

Without warning God may call us to a fast. Why does He do this? Often it is because circumstances are on the horizon that require us to be at peak performance in our walk with God.

More often than not our fasting is reactive. Subsequently, we are fasting to *undo* something or to change an old course of direction. However, fasting is best when it is *proactive*. We fast because we are prepping our body, mind and spirit to be used of God at a different level, with greater authority and power.

If we lack discipline when it comes to the Word, prayer and fasting, we will be just like the disciples. We will be woefully unprepared for the challenges ahead. The devil will defeat us every time.

"THEY COULD NOT." This phrase may be the saddest three words in the Bible. These words shout failure. Ineptitude. Weakness. Inability. My prayer is that we never hear these three bitter words spoken to or about us. On the contrary, may we be the generation that Jesus says, "THEY DID!"

17.

He Said We Would

John Stephen Akhwari represented the country of Tanzania in the
1968 Olympic marathon race in Mexico City. He qualified to run
the 26.2 mile event. Seventy-five runners started the race, 18 quit.
Of the remaining runners Akhwari finished last -- 57th out of 57.
Nineteen minutes behind number 56, Enoch Nwemba of Zambia.
The winner of the marathon had finished an hour earlier.

What happened?

Twelve miles into the race, as runners were strategically
maneuvering for position, Akhwari collided with another racer. He
fell violently to the ground. He badly cut and dislocated his knee.
He also suffered an injury to his shoulder as a result of hitting the
pavement. After receiving much needed medical attention, he got

up, wounded and in pain, and continued to run the race. At times, the pain was so intense he had to slow down to a walk, but he didn't quit, he pressed on.

The sun had already set and the last few spectators in the arena were preparing to leave when Akhwari entered the dark tunnel to the University Olympic Stadium. On his chest and back was the number 36. He was wearing a gold tank top and green shorts, proudly adorned by his nation's colors. In great pain, with his leg bandaged, he hobbled forward. As he emerged from the tunnel, the remaining crowd stood to their feet and cheered as they watched him take his final lap. Every step was difficult, but he forged ahead until he crossed the finish line. He finished the race in last place. When interviewed and asked why he continued running despite his injuries and with no chance of winning, he simply said, "My country did not send me 5,000 miles to start the race. They sent me 5,000 miles to finish the race."[26]

The same goes for us as well. God has not chosen us to merely start the race, but to finish it. Not only finish our individual race but to finish what He started.

> "It's not who starts the game that is important, but who finishes the game."
> Coach John Wooden

The famous Coach John Wooden said, "It's not who starts the game that is important, but who finishes the game."

---

[26] Wikipedia. "John Stephen Akhwari." Wikipedia.com. https://en.wikipedia.org/wiki/John_Stephen_Akhwari.

It's important how we finish. You have heard it said that people save the best for last. Well, I believe we are the last. We are the finishers. May we obey His Word and finish strong.

NOT UP FOR DEBATE

I know we have discussed this passage multiple times, but the importance of John 14:12 cannot be overstated. To say the least, it pushes people out of their comfort zone and is the focal point for many theological discussions and debate. Jesus made no mistakes. He inserted this verse to clearly outline how His followers should live and do ministry in the last days.

John 14:12,

*12 "Most assuredly, I say to you, **he who believes in Me**, the works that I do **he will do also**; and greater works than these he will do, because I go to My Father.*

One can see why this often misunderstood scripture makes theologians and scholars apprehensive. On the surface, it does seem farfetched to actually believe Christians can do the works of Christ.

Consequently, because this passage is difficult to apply to our modern era, many commentators are left to speculate on the actual meaning of Jesus' words. By the time the "experts" are done "explaining" and giving their professional opinion on what Jesus "really meant to say," this passage has very little meat left on the bone. And, for the most part, it is useless to the modern believer; therefore, rendering this text of no current usable value outside of its historical context.

Interesting to me, while the scholars are actively bloviating about why we cannot do what Jesus said we could do, I observe there is no expiration date attached to the end of this verse. Jesus' instruction and promise to His followers transcend all time and all cultures. His mandates are just as applicable to us in the 21st century as they were to the 1st-century disciples.

Furthermore, what Jesus said in John 14:12 isn't a suggestion or a recommendation, but an understood by-product of following and believing in Him. Christ envisioned His followers living this way. In fact, to not believe this will significantly affect your faith, lessen your expectations and hinder the impact your life could have.

WAS JESUS TALKING ABOUT ME?

Jesus makes it clear who qualifies and is capable of doing His works, that is… *"he who believes."* You see, the great news is that John 14:12 isn't referring to just the disciples who were present with Him, nor to an exclusive class of Christians. No, He says, *"he who believes."*

If you *have believed* then Jesus is talking about you. This verse is yours to claim. Without exception, He is saying you *can* and are *expected* to *do* what He *did."* It's that simple!

What *did* Jesus do?

Jesus left us a great example to follow. Here are a few things, a short list of some of what Jesus did:

He loved.

He taught.
184

He showed compassion to those who were hurting.

He healed the sick and opened blinded eyes.

He lifted up the underprivileged.

He made the weak strong.

He made the lepers whole by a single touch of His hand.

He caused demons to run in terror.

He dispersed life and hope to all that were willing to receive.

Jesus helped humanity everywhere He went. And it was Jesus who said, *"the works I do you shall do."*

To me, this is great news! We get to participate in God's redemptive purpose for the world. We are not just spectators.

"HE WHO BELIEVES..."

Do you believe the promises of God? Sure you do. God cannot lie. He can fulfill every promise He makes. If God said in His Word that something is possible for me to experience, then it is possible for me to experience it. His word is truth.

I want to build your faith. What Jesus said in John 14:12 is achievable for you. It is doable. You just have to believe. Did you know the *he who believes in me* statement is just as trustworthy and applicable as the following declarations Jesus made about *believing in Him.*

- *"Whoever believes in Him...shall have everlasting life."* (John 3:16)

- *"Whoever believes in me shall never thirst."* (John 6:35)

- *"Whoever believes in me ... 'Out of his heart will flow rivers of living water.'"* (John 7:38)

- *"Whoever believes in me, though he die, yet shall he live."* (John 11:25)

- *"Whoever believes in me will not remain in darkness."* (John 12:46)

Think about this for a moment. Christians everywhere are quick to embrace the wonderful blessings of those passages of scripture. Why? These statements are at the core of the gospel message, and we receive the benefit of believing; it is experiential, immediate, and explainable.

You believe then You receive.

Who wants to live in darkness? No one would resist "rivers of life." Who doesn't want to live and not die? All of the benefits listed above are a result of believing in and following Jesus.

It is worth noting that many of the same Christians who aggressively claim the blessings of the verses above are somewhat apprehensive to embrace the mandate of John 14:12. They seem to have difficulty accepting and applying this verse to their lives. Could it be that the *believing* aspect now expects something from them? In essence, it is as if they are picking and choosing which portions of the Bible they want to practice.

I am convinced, without believing this passage and its relevance in our everyday Christianity, we will not and cannot finish what Jesus asked us to do.

UNBELIEVING BELIEVERS

Leonard Ravenhill, the great preacher from the previous generation said, "One of these days some simple soul will pick up the Book of God, read it, and believe it. Then the rest of us will be embarrassed. We have adopted the convenient theory that the Bible is a Book to be explained, whereas first and foremost it is a Book to be believed (and after that to be obeyed.)" He later called this generation, "unbelieving believers."

Here is our dilemma. For the most part, Christians don't actually believe that what Jesus said is possible in our time. They have forgotten His words, *"all things are possible to him who believes"* (Mark 9:23).

A.J. Gordon said, "God does not perform His wonders in an unbelieving church that does not expect them." Perhaps inadvertently, leaders have created and cultivated a climate of unbelief in our churches. Thus, we do not see His power manifest.

If Jesus said it is possible, I'm going to believe it to be so. F.B. Meyer once said, "You never test the resources of God until you attempt the impossible."

I have made my mind up. I'm going to do it and believe God to bring about His results. If I'm guilty, then let me be guilty of daring to believe Him for greater things.

I say, let the scoffers scoff and the philosophers debate. The theologians can argue over which dispensation we are in. Those who teach and practice cessation theology can work overtime trying to validate why God no longer does what He used to do. As far as I'm concerned, the doubters can continue to doubt. None of their religious rhetoric will change my position.

> *"I'm not waiting for a move of God.*
> *I am a move of God."*
> William Booth

Here is why, I have seen sight restored to the blind, hearing to the deaf, and even large tumors disappear. I must say, my eyes have seen too much and my ears have heard too much to convince me that God cannot use us the same way He used the first disciples.

I love what William Booth, the Founder of the Salvation Army, said. "I'm not waiting for a move of God. I am a move of God." This is it! Each of us have the Kingdom of God inside of us (Luke 17:21). Everywhere we go we take His Kingdom.

I want to be one of the believing ones. I am expecting God to use me the same way He used the disciples.

It's possible. The same Holy Spirit that fell on and filled Peter, James, Mary the mother of Jesus and the others on the day of Pentecost is the same Spirit that God sends to us. There is absolutely no variation or lessening of the power, it is the same.

And because we have access to the same power they had then, we can and should accomplish what they accomplished.

> *"The works that I do, you shall do...."*
> John 14:12

18.

Time to Stand

---

*"The world needs Christians who don't tolerate the
complacency of their own lives."*
Francis Chan

How would you answer the following?

* Where do you see yourself in one year? Five years? Ten years?

* What difference have you made and ultimately, will you make on
the earth?

* What will people say at your funeral?

* What will your story be?

* How will eternity remember your contribution to Jesus' work?

* What mark are you leaving on your church, your family and your friends?

The answers you give will shed light on what your life is and will be in the days to come. As someone once said, "When it's all said and done, will you have said more than you have done?"

THE DEVIL'S LIES

As you read this, many of you believe the devil's lies. He has convinced you that your life means very little and your contribution to the Kingdom of God does not and will not matter.

These may be some of your thoughts:

"Well, I am just one person."

"I have had a difficult life. Therefore, I can't …"

"I'm too tired."

"I work too much. Besides, I won't make that big of a difference."

"I'm too old."

"You don't know me. I've done too many bad things."

"I don't know enough. I don't have anything to offer."

"I have served my time."

Wrong. Stop it. It isn't true. The devil wants you to think and talk that way. The enemy wins when you accept these statements as truth. This flawed reasoning paralyzes you and thrusts you into a dismal state of inactivity, confusion and potentially, into depression.

HERE IS THE TRUTH

Your life matters! God makes zero mistakes. You were fearfully and wonderfully made (Psalm 139:14). Do you realize how different the world would be if you were not born? You are not just valuable, you are necessary. You have a unique role to play in the lives of others and ultimately, the plan of God. Never forget that you have been strategically placed in the body of Christ as it has pleased Him (1 Corinthians 12:18). Your touch, your smile, your presence and your contribution has great significance. God wants to use you and all that you are for His glory.

Don't underestimate what God *can* do with you!

It's time to change your perspective. I encourage you to look at your life through the lens of God's unequaled grace, favor, and mercy. The God who knew what you would be like at your worse still chose to die for you and even still chooses to love you now. God knows you from top to bottom and inside and out. Your weakness does not move Him to love you less. He sees beyond your frailties and sees you complete in Him. He sees your potential.

> *Do you realize how different the world would be if you were not born?*

The time in which we live is dark and evil. God needs you. The days of watching others work for the King are over. The time of feeling unqualified and unworthy have now passed. You can no longer afford to sit on the sidelines because someone in the church offended or hurt you. Your inactivity must come to an end now.

WE LIKE TO SLEEP

Don't you love the snooze button on your alarm clock? It is my favorite feature. It's my friend. Throughout history, there have been certain inventions that were labeled extraordinary, revolutionary, live changing, or divinely inspired. There is no debate, the introduction of the "snooze button" ranks right up there with the best of them.

We are all acquainted, on some level, with the "snooze button" and how it works. This wonderful device allows you to postpone, ever so slightly, the start of your day. In essence, it affords you the sweet opportunity for a few extra minutes of much-needed sleep. The "snooze button" truly is a gift from God.

When He wrote the book of Romans, Paul was addressing a sleeping church. In Romans 13:11, he encouraged the Christians to "wake up" from their sleep and not to press the "snooze button."

Romans 13:11,
"And *do* this, knowing the time,
that now *it is* high time to ***awake out of sleep***;
for now our salvation *is* nearer
than when we *first* believed."
(emphasis added)

Regretfully, some Christians have pressed the "snooze button" and are in a state of ease and inaction. They are waiting for the perfect time to become active for God. However, there is no such thing as a "perfect time" to start serving Him. There will always be issues, unanswered questions and multiple reasons to not get involved.

I know you have heard a million times that Jesus is coming soon. You have heard it so much that it has possibly lost its meaning. But it is true. Time is running out and with growing intensity, Jesus' return is approaching. At this precise moment, the chambers of heaven echo the command for us to arise from slumber. We must awake and serve. Remember, if you don't do your part, your part does not get done.

WHAT DO I DO?

Your first step is to enlist in your local church and become actively engaged in what they are doing for the Kingdom of God. Your pastor and church leadership need you and would welcome you with open arms. You must not forget that the church you attend is God's answer regarding the issues and problems of your community. It is the hope of the city, the lighthouse and beacon of life. Your involvement will help that light to shine brighter and longer.

Remember, if you don't do your part, your part does not get done.

FEAR NO MORE

George Addair said, *"Everything you have ever wanted is on the other side of fear."* Fear is a powerful emotion. It limits. The fear of failure and the fear of the unknown paralyzes people. It robs them of the strength to move forward. I have discovered that fear is one of the main reasons believers do not become involved in God's work.

The Apostle Paul addressed fear when he wrote a letter to Timothy, his young prodigy preacher,

> *"God has not given us the spirit of **fear**,*
> *but of **power**, love and a sound mind."*
> 2 Timothy 1:7

Theodore Roosevelt, the 26th President of the United States, said, *"Believe you can and you're halfway there."*

I declare over your life that you will not be overcome with fear. In eternity past, God chose for you to be alive at this precise moment. You are not a mistake. You are not disqualified. You are able! You are a part of His master plan for the world. You were created for this precise moment.

Your church, as well as the world, is waiting for you to position yourself in the greatest army on earth. So, get up from your seat and stand, **receive your assignment, operate in your gift,** and **walk in the power of the Holy Spirit.**

> *"When I stand before God at the end of my life,*
> *I would hope that I would not have a single bit of talent left and*
> *could say, I used everything you gave me."*
> *Erma Bombeck*

STAND!

19.

"Where You Go To Church Matters"

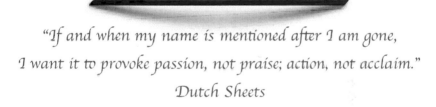

*"If and when my name is mentioned after I am gone,
I want it to provoke passion, not praise; action, not acclaim."*
Dutch Sheets

Many of us grew up in churches where we never saw nor experienced the manifest power of God first hand. It never happened. Rest assured we heard numerous sermons about what God did in the past, but rarely, if ever, did we hear about a current example of God's power. Church became a museum. It was a history lesson of all that God used to do. If our pastor mentioned a current demonstration of God's power, it was normally a story about a missionary in a country whose name we couldn't pronounce.

What followed was an unintended consequence.

The absence of God's power at the altars of our churches sent an indelible message to each of us... "there is nothing to see here." We assumed because we didn't see or experience "it" that God didn't do that type of thing anymore. Therefore, we inadvertently settled in our minds that this is normal modern day Christianity. Anything else but this kind of church experience was to be doubted, called extreme, manipulative, and very unsettling.

I don't mean to overstate reality, but a high percentage of Christians attend churches where the Church leadership, intentionally or unintentionally, have stripped the God of the universe of His power.

Church became a museum. It was a history lesson of all that God used to do.

Regretfully, particular churches and denominations have developed theological positions that teach what God gladly *used* to do and what God chooses *not to do* today. They offer a plethora of philosophical reasons why He won't do miracles now. In some instances, it seems they take great pleasure in representing the limitations of God.

In taking such a position, Church leaders have significantly weakened the body of Christ and its influence on the earth. Today, an overwhelming portion of the Church doesn't even expect the power of God to manifest in and through their lives. This is sad.

Make no mistake about it, the church you attend affects your faith. It has a direct impact on how you view God and how you manifest your Christianity to the world. Early on, I made my mind up that I would not go to a church or raise my family in a church that does not believe and teach all of God's Word.

Question: Why would you expose yourself and your family to dead faith? It makes no sense. It matters where you go to church.

THE TIME HAS COME FOR CHANGE

We are living in troubled times, and weak and unbelieving churches will be unable to offer any hope to this world. In fact, these type of churches will be completely useless.

For the sake of the world, we cannot afford any more "ordinary churches." You ask what an ordinary church is - it is a church that plays it safe, it peddles a polished gospel. It has the flare but no fire. It is routine. It is afraid to "venture out" into the spiritual, the unknown. It makes little noise and basically goes unnoticed. Its primary aim is to garner the respect of the community; it is careful to monitor expression in order not to be labeled radical, extreme, or fanatical. Its goal is to

> *You ask what an ordinary church is - it is a church that plays it safe, it pushes a polished Gospel. It has flare but no fire.*

improve your lifestyle and to service your needs as professionally as possible. They talk little of personal holiness and sacrifice.

Its reputation is the highest priority.

These churches are like the disciples who remained in the boat while Peter walked on water. They were afraid of "rocking the boat" so they stayed behind. Comfortable. Dry. Safe. Familiar.

However, it was Peter who defied reason and risked it all. He chose to believe. In return, he was the only person, besides Jesus, who ever walked on water. The disciples watched "inside" the boat as Peter experienced God's power.

Today, we need a new breed of churches. Water walking churches. Those that dare to believe for more and are willing to leave the predictable and venture out into the troubled waters, the God-zone.

NEEDED: NEW KIND OF PREACHERS

Again, it must be made clear; this is no ordinary time. The hour in which we live is critical. This is not the moment for commonplace churches, preachers and ordinary men. As Leonard Ravenhill once asked, "Where are the Elijah's of God?"

Where are the men and women of God who venture to believe, who attempt to represent Him in His fullness?

A brilliant man by the name of Albert Einstein once said, "In the middle of difficulty lies opportunity." Right now, the pain and depth of despair is at epidemic proportions. Times are tough, but it is the perfect opportunity for the Church to take her rightful place of authority and demonstrate to the world genuine love and God's unequaled manifest power.

Will this be easy? No. Nor will it be popular. We will be misunderstood, mocked, scorned and in many cases, persecuted. Rest assured that if we walk as the early church walked, we will receive the same treatment.

> *We are still talking about what they did, and it has been over 2,000 years. Wow!*

Don't let that discourage you! Take a look at what they accomplished for Jesus. We are still talking about what they did and it has been over 2,000 years. Wow!

Francis Chan correctly said, "Having faith often means doing what others see as crazy. Something is wrong when our lives make sense to unbelievers." May we live in such a way that our faith causes others to call us crazy. May they talk of how we believed God. It's time to rock the boat as Peter did.

May our prayers mirror the cry of Isaiah's heart,

> *"Oh, that You would rend the heavens!*
> *That You would come down!*
> *That the mountains might shake*
> *at Your Presence."*
> Isaiah 64:1

20.

God Needs A Body

"Give me one hundred preachers who fear nothing but sin and desire nothing but God, and I care not a straw whether they be clergymen or laymen, such alone will shake the gates of hell and set up the Kingdom of God upon the earth."
John Wesley

She was engaged to her sweetheart, Joseph. Her whole life was in front of her - marry, have kids, raise a family and be a productive member of the community. In other words, live a normal life. Little did she know that in mere moments, as a result of an extremely unusual meeting, nothing would ever be normal again! An angel approached her and said, "God needs your body."

This is remarkable. I mean, it's not every day an angel appears and says, "Hey, heaven needs you to carry a baby in your womb and nine months from now you will give birth to the Son of God, the Savior of the world." Needless to say, that kind of announcement would mess up the best of plans.

This is how Luke recorded the encounter:

Luke 1:30, 34-35,

30 *"Then the angel said to her, 'Do not be afraid, Mary, for you have found favor with God.* **31** *And behold, you will conceive in your womb and bring forth a Son, and shall call His name Jesus.'"*

34. *Then Mary said to the angel, "How can this be, since I do not know a man?"* **35** *And the angel answered and said to her, "The Holy Spirit will come upon you, and the power of the Highest will overshadow you; therefore, also, that Holy One who is to be born will be called the Son of God."*

Thankfully, here is how Mary ultimately responded after hearing the detailed plans God had for her:

*"I am the Lord's servant, **Let it be to me**
according to your word."*
Luke 1:38

Here is the million dollar question. Could Mary have refused this assignment?

She could have responded, "No, I don't want this to happen. I'm not interested." Or, "I

Was it remotely possible for Mary to have said, "No, I don't want this to happen. I'm not interested."

refuse to let you do this to me."

Instead she said, "... *Let it be to me according to your word.*"

Her response indicates that it was possible that she could have chosen not to comply with the angel's message from heaven.

What if she had said no, what then? Naturally, God would have had to find another young girl to host and carry His Son. Someone else would have to give birth to the Messiah. The hunt would have continued. Thankfully, she said, "YES! Do just as you said. Make it so. I submit to this plan."

She yielded her body for God's purpose.

JESUS NEEDED A BODY

Furthermore, God, in order to accomplish His redemptive purpose for mankind on earth, needed Jesus to have a physical body. He could not save humanity from their sin while remaining in heaven. Jesus had to take on flesh. He had to become a man. Therefore, He needed an earth suit, a body.

*"**And the Word became flesh and dwelt among us**, and we
beheld His glory, the glory as of the only begotten
of the Father, full of grace and truth."*
John 1:14

*"Therefore, when He came into the world, He said:
"Sacrifice and offering You did not desire,
But **a body You have prepared for Me**."*
Hebrews 10:5

*"Let this mind be in you which was also in Christ Jesus, 6 who, being in the form of God, did not consider it robbery to be equal with God, 7 but made Himself of no reputation, **taking the form of a bondservant, and coming in the likeness of men. 8 And being found in appearance as a man...**"*
Philippians 2:5-8

Jesus lived in our time-space dimension for thirty-three years. He was 100% man and 100% God at the same time. During His brief stay on earth, Jesus breathed this planet's air, ate the food from the ground, drank from the wells, and fished in the rivers and lakes that He created. The scriptures reveal that, after exerting Himself, He would become hungry and thirsty. His physical body would get fatigued, and therefore, He would need to rest.

Jesus displayed what it meant to be fully human. On several occasions, He demonstrated a broad range of emotions. For example, He openly wept at a friends tomb, became angry over the misuse of His Father's house, and He was greatly distressed in the garden of Gethsemane. In other situations, He showed compassion and empathy to those who were taken advantage of by society. Also, even though, He was amazed at the Centurion's faith, He was severely disappointed at the lack of faith demonstrated by His disciples.

Jesus wrapped himself in flesh. He ate, slept, and did ministry in a human body.

NOW WHAT?

Throughout the Bible, we see God has always used people to accomplish His purposes. It's just the way He does things. For example:

When God needed a REPRESENTATIVE to save the children of Israel from starvation, He used Joseph.

When He needed a DELIVERER, He called out to MOSES.

When He needed to BUILD an ark, He chose NOAH.

When He needed to SAVE a nation, HE used ESTHER.

When He needed FIRE to fall from Heaven, He appointed ELIJAH.

When He needed a GIANT exterminated, He selected DAVID.

When He needed a FORERUNNER, He tapped John the Baptist.

When He needed a SAVIOR, HE put on flesh and came.

When He needed a SPOKESPERSON for the early church, He used PETER.

When He needed an APOSTLE, He chose PAUL.

RIGHT NOW, HE NEEDS A BODY

According to Ephesian 1:22-23, Jesus is the Head of the Church, His body.

*22 "And He put all things under His feet, and gave Him to be head over all things to the church, 23 which is **His body**, the fullness of Him who fills all in all."*

One of my primary goals for this work is to help people see that God works through man, His body, to accomplish His purposes on the earth. He looks to us, His representatives, to give Him the passageway to intervene. John Wesley, the founder of the Methodist Movement, demonstrated he understood this concept when he said, "It seems God is limited by our prayer life — that He can do nothing for humanity unless someone asks Him."

Whatever you do, please do not underestimate how valuable you are to God. Your presence on the earth matters. It really does. You have a divine purpose. Your body is of utmost importance to God.

*"...Now **the body** is not for sexual immorality **but for the Lord**, and the Lord for the body."*
1 Corinthians 6:13

*"Or do you not know that **your body is the temple of the Holy Spirit** who is in you, whom you have from God, and **you are not your own**? 20 For you were bought at a price; therefore **glorify God in your body** and in your spirit, which are God's."*
1 Corinthians 6:19.

In light of the scripture above, the following truth cannot be overemphasized. Its implications are paramount:

Without us cooperating with God and yielding our body for His use, His present day work on the earth will be negatively impacted and in some places, nonexistent.

I know that concept is hard for many to grasp, but it is true. Even today this is being realized. A significant portion of the world has zero Christian influence. It's not that there are too few Christians, in fact, there are 2.2 billion of us on the earth.[27] The problem is too few Christians are willing to surrender their body to the Holy Spirit to fulfill the purpose of God.

"GOD, DO SOMETHING!"

Make no mistake; God desperately wants to help people. He sees humanity's suffering and it profoundly troubles Him. He is not oblivious to the devastation, violence, and heartache that our world is experiencing. But we want Him to do more, don't we? So, we often cry out, "God, why don't you do something! Why don't you help? Where are you?" It is at that moment, if we become still and quiet, we will hear God say, "I want to and I will. But I need your body!"

When God works in the earth, it usually comes through an obedient believer who has yielded His body for the King's purposes.

When God works in the earth, it usually comes through an obedient believer who has yielded His body for the King's purposes.

QUESTION: Do you know how important you are? Do you get it? No...do you get it? Do you really get how critical your life is to God?

---

[27] Pew Research Center. "Global Christianity - A Report on the Size and Distribution of the World's Christian Population." PewForum.org. http://www.pewforum.org/2011/12/19/global-christianity-exec/.

God is looking for a new body to use, mine and yours. 2 Chronicles 16:9,

> *"For the eyes of the Lord run to and fro throughout the whole earth, to show Himself strong on behalf of those whose heart is loyal to Him..."*

What are you allowing the Spirit to do with your BODY?

How much control does He actually have over your life? Is HE able to use your body whenever and however He pleases? Can He send your body to any place in the world? Can He count on you to say whatever He needs you to say? Does He have access to what is in your wallet? Does He have control of your interests, hobbies, and preferences?

God replies,

"I need your body!"

Christianity is not just about the Spirit being in you, but how the Spirit is using you?

Give God permission to USE YOUR BODY.

IT'S ALL IN THE PRESENTATION

The writer of Romans understood the importance of "presenting" your body to God. Not just once, but three times, Paul commands us to do so.

> *And do not present your members as instruments of unrighteousness to sin, but **present yourselves to God** as being*

*alive from the dead, and your members as **instruments of***
***righteousness** to God.*
Romans 6:13

Here it is, in plain sight. Paul is saying, *"present your body to God and allow all of you to be used as an instrument in His hands."* Have you ever thought about your body being an *instrument* in God's hands? Let Him *play* it as He wills. May your body be a tool in His hands. Allow Him to control it as He desires. Let it bring pleasure to Him.

*"...so now **present your members** as*
***slaves** of righteousness for holiness."*
Romans 6:19

Here, Paul encourages believers to, *"present their body to the Lord and become a slave for His purposes."* What was He trying to convey to his fellow believers? First and foremost, he wanted them to give themselves completely to God. Secondly, he wanted his friends to become a slave of righteousness.

Why did Paul use the metaphor of a slave? A slave has no rights; all aspects of a slave's life are under the supervision and jurisdiction of the slave owner. The answer is obvious. The slave lives to fulfill the desires of his owner.

"I beseech you therefore, brethren, by the
*mercies of God, that you **present your bodies** a living sacrifice,*
holy, acceptable to God, which is your reasonable service."
Romans 12:1

The Apostle Paul made clear what we are to give to God. *Our bodies!* Not just our soul or spirit, but our BODY. He, more than anyone, understood that God needs our bodies to accomplish His plan for the world. Without our bodies, God's work will not be done.

It was Dwight L. Moody who said, "The world has yet to see what God can do with a man fully consecrated to him. By God's help, I aim to be that man."

The Lord is looking for a body. Again I must ask, "What are you allowing the Spirit to do with your BODY?"

Just over 100 years ago Dr. Walter Wilson heard Dr. James M. Gray preach a powerful message of surrenderance. Afterwards he hurried to his room and laid prostrate before the Lord and prayed this prayer:

"My Lord, I have mistreated You all my Christian life. I have treated You like a servant. When I wanted You I called for You; when I was out to engage in some work, I beckoned You to come and help me perform my task. I have kept You in the place of a servant. I have sought to use You only as a willing servant to help me in my self-appointed and chosen work. I shall do so no more. Just now I give You this body of mine; from my head to my feet, I give it to You. I give you my hands, my limbs, my eyes and my lips, my brain; all that I am within and without. I hand it over to You for You to live in it the life that You please. You may send this body to Africa. You may send me with Your message to Tibet. You may take this body to the Eskimos. It is your body from this moment on; help yourself to it."[28]

---

[28] V. Raymond Edman, "They Found The Secret." Zondervan Publishing House, p. 123.

We should all pray this prayer with sincerity. No doubt, it will radically change our lives.

Dear friend, this is your moment. Don't allow another day to pass without presenting your body to Him.

Now is the time to lay it down at His feet.

Surrender it.

Release ownership of it.

Donate it.

Give it away.

Unconditionally sign over the deed to your life.

Make the decision now to be like Mary, the Mother of Jesus - give God permission to use your body.

PRAY THIS PRAYER NOW!

"Dear God, here is my body. Take it. All of it.
Fill me with Your Spirit. I am Yours...
I want you to use me as a choice instrument
in your precious hands. I am Your slave.
Do with me as You will. I am here to serve You. Amen!"

Now STAND UP... Be FULL OF GOD ... GO BE JESUS!

Made in the USA
Columbia, SC
26 July 2019